Picking Winning Share

Simple ways for the intelligent investor to
combine fundamental and technical analysis
to pick winners

and

How to find big profits among the bruised,
battered, or depressed stocks that nobody wants

MICK PAVEY

Published by
Ditty Box Publishing

Picking Winning Shares. Copyright © 2011 by Mick Pavey

First published in Great Britain in 2011 by
Ditty Box Publishing
(a division of Ditty Box Ltd. Reg. No. 4602831)

A CIP catalogue record for this book is available from the British Library

First Edition
Picking Winning Shares
Pavey, Mick

ISBN 978-0-9564899-0-6

I dedicate this book to my wife, Maggie. This book wouldn't exist without her love and support. For many months, she has put up with me disappearing into my office to "bash on with the book." She has also helped with proof-reading and editing, as well as being a constant sounding board for my ideas.

ACKNOWLEDGEMENTS

Valued members of my production team include: Sunny DiMartino (diagrams, typesetting, layout, proof-reading, and general advice), The MicroArts Team (cover design), Heather's Freelance and Sharon Solutions (typing and admin support). Thank you all.

I would also like to thank Ionic Information Ltd, the owners and creators of "Sharescope." This is my preferred charting software and I am grateful for their permission to use sharecope graphs, as illustrations, throughout this book. For more details on Sharescope, go to: www.sharescope.co.uk or telephone 0207-749-8500.

CONTENTS

1

IS THIS BOOK FOR YOU?

As I picked up my pen to write this chapter, the question that came into my mind was ...

Why should you buy this book?

Have you ever wondered if it is possible to make more money each year from your investing than you do from paid employment? Well, I believe the answer is yes, you can! I have achieved this in the past two years, despite now being in a higher tax bracket. How have I done this? Well, before we go any further, let me re-assure you that it is not by using any get-rich-quick scheme or taking excessive risks. Successful investing is about steady growth and letting the magic of compound interest work for you.

I believe that you, too, can learn to become a great DIY-Investor, regularly beat the markets (and the professionals), and secure your own financial future. If I can do it, so can you! This book will help you, by teaching you how to use simple techniques, combining fundamental and technical analysis. They are clearly detailed in this "how to" guide.

You'll find out:

- How to understand the key elements of a company's finances
- About the various phases of a public company's life
- How a simple strategy will enable you to pick winning shares
- Where the big winners are found
- How to use simple "wiggle watching" (technical analysis)

- Which aspects of fundamental analysis are key to success
- Why blending technical and fundamental analysis works to pick winning shares

You will also learn how to:

- Use simple systems to screen (filter) the stock market for suitable candidates
- Carry out research and create your watch list
- Monitor this watch list and decide when to "buy"
- Review your holdings and make the important "sell" decisions

1.1 My Background

I've been investing in shares for fifteen years, have no formal investing qualifications, and I haven't worked in banking or the financial service sector. Yet, despite this, I manage to regularly "beat the markets." I've done this while working as a Chartered Surveyor in the construction industry.

To put it simply, I've spent fifteen years learning as much as I can about investing, attending courses, and being mentored by some great investors: Peter Lynch, Benjamin Graham, Warren Buffet, John Neff, Ken Fisher, Jim Rogers, etc., all via their superb books and other writings. I have included some of my favourite sources of inspiration in the recommended reading list (appendix 2).

I've also done masses of my own research, created and tested my own methodical system, and put my accumulated knowledge and innovative techniques into practice. The outcome — I consistently pick winning shares. OK, so not 100% turn out to be great winners but overall, the results have been excellent.

So, why should you listen to me? Well, in recent years, running my own investments in my spare time, I've achieved the following:

- An average annual return of 46%, over the past three calendar years, in my self-invested pension plan (SIPP). As a comparison, the All-Share Index (ASX) has lost 6.3% over the same three year period.

- In the past twelve months, to 31st December 2010, using real money in an ordinary execution-only stockbroking account, I've turned £115,055 into £174,452; a gain of £59,397 (51.6%) for the calendar year. As a benchmark, during 2010, the ASX increased from 2751.0 to 3079.4, an increase of 11.9 % in the twelve months. My return of 51.6% beat the index by a massive 39.7 percentage basis points.

Oh and by the way, I paid nothing — yes "zilch" in fund management charges to anyone!

In creating this book, I have several aims. Firstly, a desire to pass on to others what I've learned, as one of my passions is education. Secondly, the prompting of one of my friends who said "wouldn't it be great if you could teach ordinary people to beat the markets!" Finally, I also like a challenge and writing a book is certainly that!

1.2 Who Is This Book For?

This "how to" book is intended for a wide audience and will benefit the following groups of people:

- Novice investors
- Experienced investors looking to improve their results
- People looking to make their money work for them and to gain financial freedom and thus free time
- People in their 40's and 50's who are late starting a pension
- Anyone needing to create a deposit to get on the property ladder
- Families wishing to provide for their children(s) school or university places
- Investment Club members
- Business owners looking for increased returns from retained earnings
- Retired people looking for better returns on their savings

1.3 How to Use This Book

Although I would like to think that you are all going to read this book avidly from cover to cover, I have to be realistic and acknowledge that each reader is going to be starting from a different point. This could be in terms of starting capital, financial knowledge, and/or experience as an investor. Some parts of this book will be of more use to you than others. To give you some pointers, the book is structured as follows:

- Chapter 2 sets out the background to the writing of the book.
- Chapters 3 to 5 will be extremely useful to beginners or intermediate investors. Experienced investors can skip straight to chapter 6, although hopefully you will skim over the preceding chapters on your way.
- In chapters 6 to 10, you'll find the core principles and strategies that I believe will help you to pick winning shares.
- The detailed "how to" parts are contained in chapters 11 to 15. You may feel the need to dip into this section from time to time, for reference, as you learn how to apply these techniques.
- In chapter 16 ("Case Studies"), you will be able to follow the simple steps that I used to pick real "winning shares," packed with graphs illustrating key points.

I find that one of the easiest ways to learn is by watching someone else and the next best thing to that is to read about real examples.

If you need any more reasons to invest in this book, then chapter 17 will convince you. Here, you'll find details of a secret (but legal) money-making system that the wealthy use to grow rich. Using it will allow you to keep your profits, without incurring large tax bills. So let's get started ...

2

WHY ANOTHER BOOK ON INVESTING?

2.1 My Story and Reasons for Writing This Book

I spent my early working years as a farm labourer and although I enjoyed the outdoor life, I knew that it wasn't for me in the long term. I simply felt that I wasn't using my brain enough and so I resolved to change my life. By going to agricultural college, I improved my position within the farming industry ending in a Farm Foreman's role, before deciding that a career change was necessary.

Fortunately, I had stayed on at school and had three 'A' levels to my name. So after some self-analysis and research of my options, I decided to study full time for a degree. "Burning my bridges" by giving up a full-time job (with overtime) to become a student on a £40/week grant was a big shock — mainly to my friends. Some of them thought that I'd lost my marbles but one or two were supportive. I, on the other hand, was very determined and motivated. With hard work, persistence, and a lot of fun along the way, I graduated with a degree at the age of 31.

Along the way, I had learned a lot about myself. I realised that I had a reasonable aptitude for analysis and that I am a "visual learner," finding it very easy to pick up concepts and ideas from diagrams, graphs, etc.

I'm not sure how I stumbled into investing, but I do remember that my first investment was in Amstrad, Alan (now Lord) Sugar's Company.

My decision to invest was based on my own observations that Amstrad's new PC's were flying off the shelves in Dixons and other retail outlets stocking them. I watched over a period of months as my shares shot up in value. I even remember gloating about my profits, as on paper I'd doubled my money. Of course, what happened next was that that share price started to drop. I re-assured myself that this would only be a temporary thing and went about my daily life. In the end, I sold my shareholding at a slight loss. Needless to say, I didn't gloat about that!

This early experience convinced me that I needed to learn more about investing. I had experienced, at first hand, the capital growth (happiness) and loss (despair) that investing can bring. I was also aware of the basic human emotions of greed (wanting the share price to carry on upwards) and fear, as it slid, snakelike, down again. It had seemed a bit like a game of snakes and ladders — except it was my (real) money at risk!

I resolved to learn more about investing and sought out books to help me improve my knowledge and skills. In the early 1990's, having now qualified as a chartered surveyor and with my farm labouring days far behind me, I set up a design company (Architects, Engineers & Surveyors). I also started my first personal pension. In hindsight, I realise that although I knew it was good to have a pension, I had no knowledge of the different types of pensions and other tax free/tax efficient forms of investing.

The next three years were spent concentrating on establishing and growing my young company. Then, one evening, opening the post and reviewing my pension statement, a horrible realisation struck me. A few minutes with a calculator and my pension folder confirmed it — my pension pot value was less than the sum of money that I'd put into it. A remarkable feat on the part of my pension fund manager, when we were in a bull market!

I knew that time was important to grow my pension but what I hadn't appreciated was the degree to which charges, initial and for ongoing management, adversely affected the performance.

Having experienced the challenges of setting up and growing my company, I resolved that I would take control on my own financial destiny. After some detailed research, I transferred my money to a self-invested pension plan (SIPP) and set about planning my future. I took control and haven't regretted it since!

Having learned a lot and with an ever-increasing desire to help others, I've decided to write this book. However, a quick trip to Waterstones, WH Smith, or online to Amazon will show you that there are vast numbers of books on investing, so how different could my book be?

2.2 What Makes This Book Different?

Over the past few years, I've collected a mass of investment books and almost without exception, they fall into two camps:

1. **Fundamental Analysis**

   These books use techniques that are based on historic analysis of a company's trading accounts. Fundamental analysis also makes use of predictions of a company's future prospects (turnover, profit, earnings per share, etc.).

2. **Technical Analysis (TA)**

   This style of investing is based on studying the patterns of share price graphs. It utilizes moving averages, trend lines, derived shapes or patterns (head & shoulders/wedges etc.), as well as secondary indicators of volume, relative strength, on-balance volume, and other more exotic-sounding things (stochastics, moving averages, convergence/divergence, etc.).

As I continued with my investing, what I realised was that, for me, the best results came from combining both fundamental and technical analysis. In 2009, my SIPP more than doubled in value — gaining in value by 142%, compared to the gain of 25.96% in the all-share index that I use as a benchmark. This was achieved by using the methods contained in this book — methods that I believe you, too, can use to beat the markets.

Now, try as I may, I can't find any books that combine the two techniques, fundamental and technical analysis, in a practical "how to" way. The task that I've set myself is to create a book that shows how to blend these techniques in a simple way that is easy to understand and follow.

7

Why am I suggesting that this book and its approach are different? Well, the techniques contained herein can be summed up as:

- Being simple to understand and follow
- Successful in both bull and bear markets
- Containing easy-to-understand key principles that are well illustrated with diagrams and graphs
- Showing a logical common sense approach that will enable the intelligent investor to create their own financial security by picking winning shares
- Providing a short cut to becoming a successful DIY-Investor,
- Including techniques that help you to know when to sell and lock in gains
- Revealing a "secret" tax free way to hold onto your profits and grow your wealth

You will find real examples dotted throughout the book which, together with the case studies in chapter 16, will convince you that there is no mystery or magic to picking winning shares. If I can do it, so can you!

2.3 The Benefits of Reading This Book

My family and friends will tell you that I am passionate about investing and it's true. However, my underlying passion is education. By investing a small amount of money (i.e. the price of this book) and applying a reasonable amount of time and determination, you can increase your knowledge and investing performance noticeably. You will gain significant benefits, including:

- Becoming a more confident DIY-Investor
- Learning how to consistently pick winning shares
- Regularly out-performing the stock market
- Confidence to take control of your financial future
- The satisfaction of consistently out-performing most professional money managers

In the next chapter, we'll look in more detail at some of the softer "touchy feely" aspects of becoming a successful DIY-Investor.

3

WHAT YOU WILL GAIN
FROM READING THIS BOOK

3.1 Understanding Yourself as an Investor

To be a successful DIY-Investor, you need to be aware of what type of person you are. Are you patient, impulsive, analytical, careless, thoughtful, or decisive?

By understanding your dominant characteristics and your dominant desires, you will have a better chance of choosing the right type of investing strategy to suit your personality and therefore to make a success. Your age will play a part and will almost certainly affect your strategy, as you focus on your financial objectives and investing horizon. It has been said that time is the "Archimedes Lever" of investing and there is no doubt that it is the key to compounding the returns on your investments. The following table illustrates clearly the leverage of time and the importance of the percentage rate of gain on the growth of your wealth:

TABLE 3.1: Compound Interest – Single Lump Sum Invested (at different rates of return)

At start: £10,000	Annual percentage gain (%)							
Year	1%	2%	3%	5%	10%	12%	15%	20%
1	10,100	10,200	10,300	10,500	11,000	11,200	11,500	12,000
2	10,201	10,404	10,609	11,025	12,100	12,544	13,225	14,400
3	10,303	10,612	10,927	11,576	13,310	14,049	15,209	17,280
4	10,406	10,824	11,255	12,155	14,641	15,735	17,490	20,736
5	10,510	11,041	11,593	12,763	16,105	17,623	20,114	24,883
6	10,615	11,262	11,941	13,401	17,716	19,738	23,131	29,860
7	10,721	11,487	12,299	14,071	19,487	22,107	26,600	35,832
8	10,829	11,717	12,668	14,775	21,436	24,760	30,590	42,998
9	10,937	11,951	13,048	15,513	23,579	27,731	35,179	51,598
10	11,046	12,190	13,439	16,289	25,937	31,058	40,456	61,917
11	11,157	12,434	13,842	17,103	28,531	34,785	46,524	74,301
12	11,268	12,682	14,258	17,959	31,384	38,960	53,503	89,161
13	11,381	12,936	14,685	18,856	34,523	43,635	61,528	106,993
14	11,495	13,195	15,126	19,799	37,975	48,871	70,757	128,392
15	11,610	13,459	15,580	20,789	41,772	54,736	81,371	154,070
16	11,726	13,728	16,047	21,829	45,950	61,304	93,576	184,884
17	11,843	14,002	16,528	22,920	50,545	68,660	107,613	221,861
18	11,961	14,282	17,024	24,066	55,599	76,900	123,755	266,233
19	12,081	14,568	17,535	25,270	61,159	86,128	142,318	319,480
20	12,202	14,859	18,061	26,533	67,275	96,463	163,665	383,376
21	12,324	15,157	18,603	27,860	74,002	108,038	188,215	460,051
22	12,447	15,460	19,161	29,253	81,403	121,003	216,447	552,061
23	12,572	15,769	19,736	30,715	89,543	135,523	248,915	662,474
24	12,697	16,084	20,328	32,251	98,497	151,786	286,252	794,968
25	12,824	16,406	20,938	33,864	108,347	170,001	329,190	953,962
26	12,953	16,734	21,566	35,557	119,182	190,401	378,568	1,144,755
27	13,082	17,069	22,213	37,335	131,100	213,249	435,353	1,373,706
28	13,213	17,410	22,879	39,201	144,210	238,839	500,656	1,648,447
29	13,345	17,758	23,566	41,161	158,631	267,499	575,755	1,978,136
30	13,478	18,114	24,273	43,219	174,494	299,599	662,118	2,373,763

From this table, the most striking feature is the combined benefits of compounding and higher rates of growth. You can see that if we invest £10,000 in a savings account, say earning 3%, and keep the interest invested (i.e. compounding), it will grow to £24,273 over 30 years. Taking the same amount and achieving a 12% average growth rate (this being the long-term average of the stock market), our £10,000 will grow to become £299,599. This gives us 11.34 times more money over the 30-year timeframe (1,134% if you prefer percentages). This is the "reward" for taking the "risk" of investing in the stock market, rather than securing your capital in a savings account, at a lower rate of growth (interest).

Just as important as time is the principle of regular investment. If you can invest regular sums (say £50 to £100 per month) then the compounding accelerates rapidly and can lead to solid investment returns over the medium to long term.

3.2 What Are Your Objectives?

It always helps to clearly identify your reasons for investing and the goal(s) you are setting yourself. Common aims can include one or more of the following:

- Clearing the mortgage
- Saving for university or school fees for your children
- Creating a deposit to buy your first home with
- To have financial independence and 'free time'
- Providing for a comfortable retirement
- Clearing debts

Whatever your objectives or investment goals, write them down. More importantly, set yourself target dates for them. Go on… write them down now. Make them real!

My investment goals are….	I will achieve them by (date)…
1.	
2.	
3.	
4.	
5.	
6.	
7.	

If you like to put figures into your plans, you may want to go over to our website at www.diy-investors.com, where you will find some helpful spreadsheets. These are available as free downloads, to help you create your own investment plan.

3.3 Active or Passive?

Most investors quickly work out their preferred style of investing, the two main types being active or passive. It often depends on your characteristics and almost always is influenced by the stage of your life and your other time commitments.

For investors without much time or who are of a very cautious nature, the range of passive investment choices will include:

• Company or stakeholder pension plans (with or without contributions from your employer)
• Index funds – tracking popular stock market indices in the UK or around the world

- Commodity fund indices (e.g. oil, gold, or grain)
- Unit trust funds
- Investment trusts (traded like shares on the stock market)
- Government bonds (gilts)
- Corporate bonds (issued by quoted stock market companies)
- Banks and building societies (this is really parking your money!)

The more ambitious and confident DIY-Investor, prepared to put in a reasonable amount of time, will often use one, two, or more of the following "active" approaches:

- Owning shares in individual companies
- ETF's (exchange traded funds) – these can be in a broad basket of shares or commodities, or individual commodities
- Options
- CFD's (contracts for difference)
- Spread betting

This book is intended for those investors who wish to actively manage their own investments. Specifically, it is aimed at those who wish to buy and hold shares in publicly-quoted companies with the intention of holding them for the medium to long term (three months to three+ years).

3.4 So, Do You Want to DIY?
If, like me, you want to be a DIY-Investor, what do you need?

Well, given that you've taken a long, hard look at yourself and decided you have the right characteristics and determination, the following list covers the essential requirements:

- PC, with broadband internet access.
- An on-line stockbroking account (this can be an ordinary trading account or a self-select Maxi ISA or SIPP). I have all three.
- Share price graphing software. This can be a stand-alone software package, with live or 'end of day' share price feeds or an on-line free utility, often with delayed share prices. You may wish to go over to www.diy-investors.com to find some useful links to

providers of graphing software.

- A journal or large A4 "page to a day" diary will prove invaluable. Use this to record your activities, thoughts, analysis, and emotions as you go along. The best way to learn is to understand what works best for you and of crucial importance is to learn from your mistakes. In the first five years of my investing, I found that the errors I made were usually a result of rushing in to buy a share that was being touted by the "experts" in the financial press or on-line as a "buy" or "strong buy." More of this later.
- You will also need an A4 lever arch file to retain and organise your contract notes, portfolio valuations, correspondance, etc. Good record keeping is essential for tax purposes — whether you're doing your own returns or paying someone else to do this!

3.5 Now You're Ready to Begin—Or Are You?

The impatient investor will now be raring to go but before you launch headlong into the world of DIY Investing, a bit of preparation is required and, dare I say it, a bit more education. No, I don't mean GCSE's or 'A' levels but I do mean:

- Read several books – I know you've already shown that commitment by buying and reading this book but read several books. Learn from others, particularly the investing "masters" Benjamin Graham, Warren Buffet, Philip Fisher, Peter Lynch, Jim Rogers, John Neff, Jim Slater, etc. (see the recommended reading list, contained in appendix 2).
- Use the free resources available on the internet, including research tools, stock screening filters, free company (downloadable) half and full-year reports, research notes, etc.
- Join bulletin boards to find out what others are thinking but beware of taking too much notice!

If you're really struggling with confidence or would like more help and assistance, consider joining (or forming) an investment club. However, for people like me who want to be independent and do their own thing, there really is no substitute for the DIY approach!

3.6 Your Advantage as an "Amateur"

In my view, your financial future is too important to leave to other people. If you want to keep control then DIY investing is the best way.

So what are the advantages of the DIY approach? Well to my mind, there are four very good reasons:

1. **You avoid fund management charges.** These can be anywhere between 1% and 3% per year (based on your portfolio value). These apply whether your fund value goes up or down. Yes, if your fund value drops, you still pay the fee — it is not performance related.

    To consider the affect of this, consider the table (3.2) on the following page...

Table 3.2: Your Advantage as a DIY-Investor (Avoiding Annual Management Charges)

At Start: £10,000 DIY-Investor		Professionally Managed (with Annual Charges)				
Year	12% Annual Growth	12% Growth Rate, 3% Man. Charge				
		Start of Year	Growth (12%)	Before Charges	Charges (3%)	C/Fwd
1	11,200	10,000	1,200	11,200	336	10,864
2	12,544	10,864	1,304	12,168	365	11,803
3	14,049	11,803	1,416	13,219	397	12,822
4	15,735	12,822	1,539	14,361	431	13,930
5	17,623	13,930	1,672	15,602	468	15,134
6	19,738	15,134	1,816	16,950	508	16,441
7	22,107	16,441	1,973	18,414	552	17,862
8	24,760	17,862	2,143	20,005	600	19,405
9	27,731	19,405	2,329	21,734	652	21,082
10	31,058	21,082	2,530	23,612	708	22,903
11	34,785	22,903	2,748	25,652	770	24,882
12	38,960	24,882	2,986	27,868	836	27,032
13	43,635	27,032	3,244	30,276	908	29,367
14	48,871	29,367	3,524	32,892	987	31,905
15	54,736	31,905	3,829	35,733	1,072	34,661
16	61,304	34,661	4,159	38,821	1,165	37,656
17	68,660	37,656	4,519	42,175	1,265	40,910
18	76,900	40,910	4,909	45,819	1,375	44,444
19	86,128	44,444	5,333	49,778	1,493	48,284
20	96,463	48,284	5,794	54,078	1,622	52,456
21	108,038	52,456	6,295	58,751	1,763	56,988
22	121,003	56,988	6,839	63,827	1,915	61,912
23	135,523	61,912	7,429	69,341	2,080	67,261
24	151,786	67,261	8,071	75,333	2,260	73,073
25	170,001	73,073	8,769	81,841	2,455	79,386
26	190,401	79,386	9,526	88,912	2,667	86,245
27	213,249	86,245	10,349	96,594	2,898	93,697
28	238,839	93,697	11,244	104,940	3,148	101,792
29	267,499	101,792	12,215	114,007	3,420	110,587
30	£299,599	110,587	13,270	123,857	3,716	**£120,141**
				Total Management charges (@3%) =		**£42,833**

If you were ever in any doubt about the merits of being a DIY-Investor, Table 3.2 (opposite) should help you make your mind up. There are three key points to take from this:

- The left-hand column shows that a DIY-Investor, achieving an average of 12% over a 30-year timeframe, will turn £10,000 into £299,599.
- The same £10,000, invested with a professional fund manager (charging 3% of the fund value per year, as a management charge) will be worth £120,141 — a whopping loss to your finances of £179,458 (£299,599 less £120,141).
- For achieving this average performance, the management charges, at 3% over the 30-year period, are £42,833. This represents over four times the amount you originally invested! To put it another way, by taking this annual 3% charge, the total charge of £42,833 costs you £179,458 in "lost" wealth accumulation.

2. **You avoid initial charges.** Normal practice with stockbrokers and professional fund managers is that they skim off 3% to 5% *before* they invest your money.

   Again, to consider the affect of this, consider Table 3.3 (following page). This time, we'll assume that in addition to the £10,000 lump sum at the start, you manage to save another £50 per month — adding £600 per year, from the start of year two, to your investment fund.

Table 3.3: Your Advantage as a DIY-Investor (Avoiding Initial Fees and Management Charges)

At Start: £10,000 + £600/year DIY-Investor		At Start (Managed): £10,000 less 3% = £9,700 plus £600 per year less 3% = £582 added each year professionally managed (with annual charges)				
Year	12% Annual Growth	12% Growth Rate, 3% Initial Fee				
		Start of Year	Growth (12%)	Before Charges	Charges (3%)	C/Fwd
1	11,200	9,700	1,164	10,864	326	10,538
2	13,144	11,120	1,334	12,454	374	12,081
3	15,321	12,663	1,520	14,182	425	13,757
4	17,760	14,339	1,721	16,060	482	15,578
5	20,491	16,160	1,939	18,099	543	17,556
6	23,550	18,138	2,177	20,315	609	19,705
7	26,976	20,287	2,434	22,722	682	22,040
8	30,813	22,622	2,715	25,337	760	24,576
9	35,111	25,158	3,019	28,178	845	27,332
10	39,924	27,914	3,350	31,264	938	30,326
11	45,315	30,908	3,709	34,617	1,039	33,578
12	51,353	34,160	4,099	38,260	1,148	37,112
13	58,115	37,694	4,523	42,217	1,267	40,951
14	65,689	41,533	4,984	46,517	1,395	45,121
15	74,171	45,703	5,484	51,187	1,536	49,652
16	83,672	50,234	6,028	56,262	1,688	54,574
17	94,312	55,156	6,619	61,775	1,853	59,921
18	106,230	60,503	7,260	67,764	2,033	65,731
19	119,577	66,313	7,958	74,271	2,228	72,042
20	134,527	72,624	8,715	81,339	2,440	78,899
21	151,270	79,481	9,538	89,019	2,671	86,348
22	170,022	86,930	10,432	97,362	2,921	94,441
23	191,025	95,023	11,403	106,426	3,193	103,233
24	214,548	103,815	12,458	116,273	3,488	112,785
25	240,894	113,367	13,604	126,971	3,809	123,162
26	270,401	123,744	14,849	138,593	4,158	134,435
27	303,449	135,017	16,202	151,219	4,537	146,683
28	340,463	147,265	17,672	164,936	4,948	159,988
29	381,919	160,570	19,268	179,839	5,395	174,443
30	£428,349	175,025	21,003	196,028	5,881	**£190,148**
				Total Management charges (@3%) =		**£63,610**

Looking just at Table 3.3 (opposite), there are three main points that arise:

- The left-hand column shows that you, as a DIY-Investor, achieving an average of 12% over a 30-year timeframe, will turn £10,000 plus regular investments of £600 per year (a total of £28,000 invested) into £428,349. This represents a cumulative gain of £400,349 (1,429%).
- The same £10,000, invested with a professional fund manager (charging 3% of the fund value per year, as a management charge and 3% on your £600 added annually), will be worth £190,148 — leaving a whopping hole in your potential wealth of £238,201 (£428,349 less £190,148).
- Also, note that the management charges are £63,610, over the 30-year timeframe.

Comparing tables 3.1, 3.2, and 3.3, what strikes me are the following points:

- Start investing as early as you can — let time work in your favour.
- To maximise your gains, adopt a DIY-Investors approach (avoiding both initial fees and ongoing management charges). You might consider that you are paying yourself these charges!
- It's worth taking the time to improve your investing skills. From Table 3.1, it is clear that a 1% improvement in performance is worth a lot when compounding is taken into consideration.

Now, if the professionals outperformed the stock market (which you could copy by investing passively via index funds) by a sensible margin, then perhaps their charges would be seen to be reasonable. In reality, most professionals don't achieve this — not surprising perhaps, bearing in mind how much of your money they've taken in charges!

This leads to the first of our DIY-Investors rules…

DIY-Investors Rule No. 1 –*Your biggest advantage as a DIY-Investor is avoidance of management fees and charges!*

---

3. **You can use any special knowledge that you have.** Now, we're not talking about insider trading or anything illegal here. We're talking about using one or more of the following:

   • Knowledge of the industry/sector of the economy that you work in
   • Trends in lifestyle that you observe (e.g. technological innovation/evolution – mobile phones, flat screen TVs, smart phones etc.)
   • Changes in retail trends (what stores are thriving/expanding, etc.)
   • Observing changes in travel/holiday trends
   • Being generally observant of the world around you

4. **Independent thinking.** In many professional organisations, fund managers have to stick to lists of "approved shares," where their own analysts have provided the research. The key part here is that the research function is separated from the investment decision. Perhaps this is why there tends to be a "fear of failure" within some members of the professional fund managing fraternity. This aspect was discussed, from an informed insiders perspective, by Peter Lynch in his excellent book *Beating the Street* first published in 1993.

   The "out-performance" that comes from independent thinking and following a sound investment strategy is apparent from studying the great investors such as Benjamin Graham, Warren Buffet & Charlie Munger, Peter Lynch, Jim Rogers, etc.

So what tools, knowledge, and techniques do we need as keen DIY-Investors in order to succeed? Well, before we go into that, we'll take a quick look at how a company works and the key aspects of corporate finance.

If you are familiar with this, please skip ahead to chapter 5.

4

UNDERSTANDING COMPANY FINANCES

In this chapter, we'll look at the key financial points that you need to know and where to find the information in a company's accounts. For those of you who are familiar with accountancy and/or company accounts, you may prefer to skip this chapter.

4.1 Simplifying How a Business Works

There are three main financial components to business accounts: profit & loss, balance sheet, and cash flow. These apply to sole traders, partnerships, and businesses — both private and public. In reality, they also affect our individual household finances too.

Profit & Loss (or P&L)

Put simply, profit or loss is what's left from income (or turnover) after direct costs and overheads (or "fixed costs") are deducted. This figure gives trading profit (or loss) and is called net profit (loss) before tax. The P&L account covers a period of time — usually 6 or 12 months for UK registered public companies. In America, companies have to submit accounts every three months, so information available to investors is more up-to-date. Overheads would include office staff, premises-related expenses, accounting and legal fees, etc. All of these are paid, regardless of the level of turnover — hence the term "fixed costs."

It is important to note the importance that valuations can play within company accounts. For some companies such as miners, stocks are a physical commodity that will be only too obvious i.e. materials in a big heap! However, other sectors and industries will also have stocks. For example, retailers like M&S or Next, will have inventories (the retailers' term for stock) which will include unsold garments. These can quickly lose their value, for example if fashion changes, leading to massive "write offs." In the technology sector, items (e.g. micro-chips) can quickly become out-of-date (obsolescent).

> **DIY-Investors Rule No. 2** – *Watch out for rising inventory or stock levels. This can mean the company can't sell its product!*

Balance Sheet
The balance sheet is a "snapshot" of the assets and liabilities of the company — taken on the last day of the accounting period. In the UK the balance sheet is typically laid out, in a vertical format, as follows:

ASSETS
Non-Current Assets (which may include):
    Property, plant, and equipment
    Intangible assets
    Restricted cash
    Deferred tax assets
Current Assets (which may include):
    Inventories
    Trade and other receivables
    Cash and cash equivalents
    Assets classified as held for sale
Income Tax Assets
Total Assets

LIABILITIES
Non-Current Liabilities (which may include):
    Borrowings (long-term)
    Retirement benefit obligations
    Provisions
    Deferred tax liabilities
Current Liabilities (which may include):
    Borrowings (short-term)

Trade & other payables
Provisions
Income tax liabilities
Total Liabilities

Total Assets less Total Liabilities............... 'A' [balances 'B' (below)]

Equity
Shareholders' equity
Total called up share capital
Share premium
Other reserves
Retained earnings
Total Equity attributable to shareholders.... 'B' [balances 'A' (above)]

Figures are also given from the previous balance sheet for comparative purposes. These are dated at the end of the previous accounting period, for annual accounts, or for the same six-month period in the prior year, for interim accounts.

The key points that you need to pick out from a balance sheet are:

• Cash and cash items (e.g. marketable securities/investments)
• Debt (long-term and short-term borrowings)

Compare both of these to the previous balance sheet figures. If the cash is going up and the long-term debt is going down, then it shows an improving situation. Conversely, if borrowings are increasing and cash is going down, then things are getting worse.

Net cash is calculated by subtracting long-term debt from the cash. A useful calculation is to divide the net cash by the number of shares issued to find the net cash per share.

Occasionally when analysing a company, you find a hidden gem. An example of this would be a company that has a big chunk of the share price sitting as cash on the balance sheet. This effectively reduces the cost that you are paying for your share of the business. One very good example that I spotted in 2009 was GTL Resources; see box below.

GTL Resources (Epic: GTL)

By Spring 2009, GTL had been on my radar screen for some while. As a depressed share, its shareprice graph had been in a downtrend for some years. It had opened its ethanol-producing plant in December 2006 (when the shareprice was 185p) but had been beset with various problems and poor commodity margins during 2007 & 2008. On 5th March 2009, with its shareprice at 11.5p, an RNS announcement by the company stated that it had increased production to the nameplate 100-million-gallon-per-annum level (from 50 mgpa). This was followed by an individual investor making a large purchase, on 11th March, with the shareprice at 10.25p.

My interest was now heightened and with the year end (31st March) approaching, I was keeping a very close watch on the price action, via Sharescope. The GTL graph seemed fairly quiet during April, the share price sitting at 9.0p from 3rd to 22nd April. However, on 6th May 2009, GTL came to life, closing up 3.75p (34%) on massive volume of 4.96 million shares (note: the total number of shares issued = 31.99 million, so over 15% of the shares had changed hands in one day). The explanation came on 2nd June 2009, when an RNS announcement made it clear that Gartmore Investment Ltd had increased its holdings, to exceed 20% of the issued share capital — the transaction date being 6th May.

This action took the share price through the resistance (downtrend) line, as can be seen on the following graph...

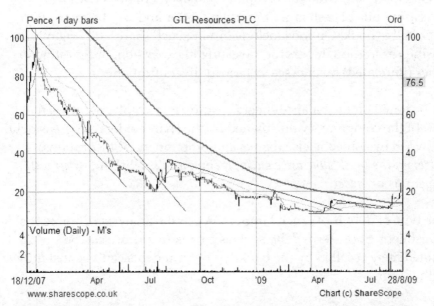

Fig. 4.1: GTL Resources – Start of the Turnaround (Spring 2009)

When the preliminary (unaudited) annual results for the year ended 31st March 2009 were announced on 17th June 2009 (with the shareprice at 13.0p), I was amazed to see that in the financial highlights, GTL had 16p cash per share plus another 19.7p restricted cash at its subsidiary IRE. When the audited annual report was released on 24th August 2009, with the price now at 16.0p, I could see from the first two photographs in the report that this modern ethanol plant was effectively available for free. The next day, 25th August, I made my initial purchase (at 17.0p), knowing that with a total of 35p in cash (16p at GTL + another 19p restricted cash), the likelihood was that GTL would be an excellent investment.

All of this information and the share price action resided in the public domain and was easily available to the DIY-Investor, all you needed to do was act!

In general terms, what the company management does with an increasing pile of cash is an important matter and will be referred to later in this book. Options include buying back shares, buying other businesses in the same sector, investing in expansion, or investing in other (unrelated) businesses — termed diversification.

Also shown on the balance sheet is equity. Put simply, equity is the part of the company's value owned by the shareholders, whereas debt is owned by someone else (banks and other financial institutions). *Note: on the bank's balance sheet, a company's debt (liability) will appear as an asset.*

The type of debt is of crucial importance in the analysis of a potential investment. Short-term debt, such as a bank overdraft, can be immediately recalled by the bank. Long-term debts can't be instantly withdrawn.

The ratio of (shareholders') equity to debt is an important ratio and shows the financial strength of the company. It is generally considered that a 75% equity to 25% debt ratio represents a strong and stable balance sheet. The reverse, 25% equity to 75% debt, would generally suggest a much weaker balance sheet. Comparison of these ratios over a series of three or four balance sheets (at six monthly intervals) can quickly alert you to improving, or deteriorating, financial circumstances of the company under scrutiny.

Assets

Assets, represented by their "book value" on the balance sheet, can be seriously undervalued. This is particularly so for companies (e.g. natural resources) with assets in the form of raw materials in the ground.

Also, bear in mind that depreciation (a cost item on the P&L account) reduces the value of an asset. Eventually, the asset may only have a "nominal" value on the balance sheet. At face value, the balance sheet (of an established company) may effectively "hide" the true value of the company's assets.

An expanding company that purchases assets (e.g. shares in another company or even the whole company) carries the value of the cost of purchase that exceeds the book value (on the target company's balance sheet) as "goodwill." This can be depreciated and, in times of financial turmoil, this goodwill can be "written off." This writing off, done at the director's discretion, shows as a cost in the P&L and has the effect of reducing (punishing) earnings for the period — frequently turning a profit into a loss.

It's also important to be aware that some items (e.g. depreciation and writing down goodwill) are "non-cash" costs in the P&L. Hence the importance of the cash flow statement in the accounts. Financial results, showing a loss but with strong cash flow, are worthy of a closer look.

Cash Flow
The cash-flow statement in the accounts shows how the profit (or loss) from the P&L is reconciled with the cash position.

Amongst other things, it will show

- Non-cash costs (depreciation, goodwill write downs, etc.)
- Cash injected into the business (loans, share issues, etc.)
- Cash withdrawn from the business (loan repayment, dividends, etc.)
- Opening and closing cash positions

Again, comparisons are given to the previous (equivalent) time period, enabling at a glance the trend to be assessed.

Looking at out-of-favour or depressed companies, I particularly look for improvements in positive cash flow, particularly when accompanied by a low profit (or even a loss) on a P&L statement. This positive cash flow will, in the normal course of events, lead to a turnaround, or substantially improved prospects, for the company.

> ***Entertainment One (Epic: ETO):***
> In summer 2009, ETO represented a very good example of the difference between P&L and cash flow. Its results for the year ended 31st March 2009, released 24th June 2009, had shown a reported pre-tax loss of £31.0m (2008: loss = £7.7m), whereas the positive operating cash flow of £35.9m (up from £28.7m in 2008), showed a different story. ETO is covered more fully in chapter 16 ("Case Studies").

In our goal of "picking winning shares," we aim to look for clues to help us identify future winners and cash generation is key to this.

Notes to the Accounts
Tucked away, behind the P&L, balance sheet, and cash-flow statement, you will find the notes to the accounts. These are numbered and cross references to these are contained in the P&L statement and balance sheet.

Particular items to look for in the notes include:

- Details of inventory/stock levels
- Production output levels (for industrial, mining companies)
- Sales levels (growth or decline)
- Growing or shrinking costs of production
- Notes indicating special factors affecting the company's fortunes
- Explanation of growing (or reducing) overheads
- Details of tax paid (or re-claimed)
- Borrowing details – including length of loans, interest rates, and timing of payments
- Special provisions (the "write-offs" that I mentioned earlier)
- Details of any financing or re-financing – both of these can affect how debt is structured (which we want to know)

4.2 Differences Between a Private and Public Company
The key difference between private and public limited companies is who can own shares in the company.

Private Companies

Ownership of private company shares is restricted and details of these restrictions are usually covered in a shareholder agreement. No ordinary member of the public would normally be able to buy shares in a private company.

Similarly, if you came to own shares in a private company (e.g. through an inheritance), restrictions on how you can dispose of them apply. You become bound by the terms of the shareholders agreement.

Private Companies that are set up with the intention of going public, offer the sophisticated/expert investor potential for large rewards. These investments carry higher risk and are beyond the scope of this book. However, there are opportunities, through Venture Capital Trusts (VCT's) to take a stake in a 'basket' of start up or early stage private companies, some of which may 'go public'. These VCT's are publicly traded collective investment schemes that provide tax efficient ways for private investors to participate in start up or small expanding companies.

Public Companies

Shares in public companies can be bought and sold on the stock exchange. Companies select which stock exchange they wish to "list" on. This "listing" is subject to the rules of the chosen stock exchange. In the UK, the two main stock exchanges are the London Stock Exchange (LSE) and the Alternative Investment Market (AIM). Many companies choose to list on more than one market. For example, Western Coal (previously Western Canadian Coal) is dual listed on AIM and the Toronto Stock Exchange (TSX).

One of the key aspects of a quoted (i.e. publicly quoted) company is the market capitalisation (MCAP for short) which is simply the number of shares issued multiplied by the share price, e.g. a company with 35.8 million shares issued and a quoted stock price of £2.50 per share will have a capitalization (MCAP) of £89.5 million.

The MCAP is a widely quoted figure, indicating the size of a company. It is also widely used, when combined with other factors, to create ways to measure of the value of a company.

29

Common Methods of Valuing a Company
Whole books are written on this subject, but here I'm restricting discussion to (arguably) the most common ones, which are:

- PSR – Price-to-sales ratio
- PBV – Price-to-book value
- PTBV – Price-to-tangible book value
- PCF – Price-to-cash flow
- DY – Dividend yield
- PE – Price-to-earnings ratio (sometimes called PER)
- PEG – Price-to-earnings growth

Some of these can be expressed on a historic or prospective (forward looking) basis. Normal convention is that a prospective ratio has (pr) following the abbreviation. So, PSR becomes PSR(pr), for prospective price-to-sales ratio. Similarly you may see (h) following the abbreviation, referring to historic figures. In both cases the price refers to the current price at which the company, as a whole or per share, is priced at.

For example (looking at price to earnings, PE):

Company X has reported earnings of 25p per share in the last annual accounts and has a current price of £2.50 per share. The PE is calculated as:

$$\frac{2.50}{0.25} = 10 \quad \text{[PE(h) is 10]}$$

If the current consensus of analysts' estimates gives projected earnings for the current year of 30p per share, then the prospective PE is calculated as:

$$\frac{2.50}{0.30} = 8.33 \quad \text{[PE(pr) is 8.33]}$$

It also follows, in this example, that analysts believe that the company can grow its earnings by 20% (from 25p to 30p per share). This is the earnings growth rate.

Let's take a quick look at the rest of the valuation measures listed above.

PBV (Price-to-Book Value)
The book value is found from the balance sheet. In essence, it is calculated by subtracting all liabilities from the assets and dividing by the number of shares in issue. Note: If the number of shares has changed during the accounting period, then a weighted average is used for the calculation.

A further complication can arise if preference shares have been issued. These rank ahead of (are more senior to) the common or ordinary shares that represent public ownership. Their value is therefore subtracted to get to book value, for the above calculation.

PTBV (Price-to-Tangible Book Value)
The book value used above will include intangibles (goodwill, trade or brand names, etc.). By excluding these from the calculation, we arrive at tangible book value. The calculation, thereafter, is the same as for PBV (above).

One important aspect of PTBV is that for PTBV values below 1.0, if the company was sold and the proceeds distributed to the shareholders, you should receive more than the price of the shares. The essence of "value investing," uses a range of measures like this to seek winning shares. Investors anticipate that future share price growth will arise from wider recognition of this "undervaluing" of a company's assets.

PCF (Price-to-Cash Flow)
Cash flow is, as you would expect, to be found from the cash-flow statement.

The cash-flow statement adjusts the earnings, to add back the non-cash costs (like depreciation). It also shows the cost of new capital expenditure (which will be depreciated in future accounting periods), arriving at an increase or decrease in the cash position over the accounting period. The change, start to finish, is the cash flow — again usually expressed on a per-share basis. Cash flow, after taking account of normal capital expenditure, is sometimes called free cash flow.

The subject can be further complicated by investments that the company may make. For example, a company may invest (from its cash reserves) in another business. The investment (shares in the business) will sit on the balance sheet as an asset (short- or long-term asset, depending on how marketable the shares are). Thus the company's investing activities can appear to distort the cash-flow statement. Similarly, changes in money owed by (or to) the company, will appear to distort the cash-flow figures.

PSR (Price-to-Sales Ratio)

Sales, in this context, is the turnover of the company and is a reflection of the activity level of the business. Companies like to be growing sales constantly but fluctuations can arise from a variety of factors including:

- Glitches in production (technical, accident, weather etc.)
- Irregular increase/decrease in sales price
- Changes in demand for product (recession, competition, obsolescence, etc.)

However, the turnover (sales) of the company is, arguably, the most important figure — being the top line from which deductions are made to get to gross profit, net profit, earnings per share, etc. We'll come back to this later, in chapters 9 and 16 of this book.

If our Company X has sales per share of £6.50 (Annual sales divided by the number of issued shares in the company), then its PSR is calculated as:

$$\frac{£2.50}{£6.50} = 0.38 \qquad [PSR = 0.38]$$

Many people consider that the price-to-sales ratio is a good measure of the popularity of a company with investors. This can be guaged by comparing the company PSR with other similar companies (in the same sector).

DY (Dividend Yield)

Dividends are cash paid to shareholders from profits (or retained profits) and are one very good reason to invest in shares of a quoted company (i.e. to create an income). Many mature companies produce a steady (usually increasing) stream of income for their owners.

The dividend yield is calculated simply by dividing the annual dividend per share by the current price and multiplying by 100 to give a percentage figure.

So if our fictitious company with a current share price of £2.50/share has paid dividends of 10p in the past year, then the DY is calculated as:

$$\frac{0.10}{2.50} \quad \times 100 = 4\% \quad [DY = 4\%]$$

If analysts are predicting dividends for the current year of 11p (a 10% growth in dividends) then the prospective DY(pr) is calculated as:

$$\frac{0.11}{2.50} \quad \times 100 = 4.4\% \quad [DY(pr) = 4.4\%]$$

PEG (Price-to-Earnings Growth)
This ratio, originally devised by the investment guru Jim Slater, is calculated by dividing the growth rate into the PE ratio. For example, we will use our fictitious company (with PE of 10) and reported earnings of 25p per share. If we assume that the company's earnings had increased by 15% in the previous year, then the calculation would be:

$$\frac{PE}{(EPS \text{ growth})} \quad \frac{10}{15} \quad = 0.66 \quad [PEG = 0.66]$$

the smaller this gets the better

If, looking ahead, the earnings are expected (as stated earlier) to grow at 20%, then the prospective PEG would be:

$$\frac{10}{20} \quad = 0.50 \quad [PEG(pr) = 0.50]$$

Generally, followers of this method believe that any figure below 1.0 is OK, below 0.75 is good, and at a PEG of 0.50 or below is very good.

This valuation method aims to ensure you are paying a reasonable price for the growth in earnings and is particularly suited to growth companies (generally those in the first 10–15 years of their "public" life).

Market Sentiment

How the market, i.e. the investors (public and professional), view a company can radically affect the valuation of that company, regardless of what method of valuation is used. This is all too evident when a company suffers some setback or issues a piece of bad news. The plunging share price is a reaction, out of fear, to the setback.

Similarly, whole markets can be affected. The atrocious 9/11 terrorist attacks on the twin towers in New York caused stock markets around the world to drop suddenly — taking many weeks to recover. Similar falls came about in late 2008, arising from the worldwide banking crisis. Government intervention to bail out troubled banks, termed quantitative easing, coupled with emergency reduction of interest rates, reduced the effect of this fall. Subsequently the stock markets recovered, although some would say perhaps artificially.

Again, whole books have been written on the subject of fear and greed in the stock markets. As DIY-Investors, I believe we do well to be aware of market sentiment generally and in particular develop an awareness of your own "market sentiment" (i.e. feelings of fear or greed).

Before I begin to set out my detailed strategy for picking winning shares, we'll examine the typical life span of a public company. You need to be aware of this when assessing a potential investment candidate.

5

THE LIFE SPAN OF A PUBLIC COMPANY

Public companies begin their lives in three different ways. Firstly, private companies that are trading "float" (by selling a proportion of their shares publicly) to raise funds to expand, or develop a product or technology.

The second group represents companies that raise funds to purchase an asset (perhaps mining or mineral exploration rights) which they then seek to exploit commercially.

The third group are investment companies where funds are raised with the purpose of buying shares in other companies, public or private, in a particular market (e.g. oil exploration/production) or a specific geographical location (e.g. China or India).

Sometimes shares are "placed" with financial institutions or issued to the public via an initial public offering, commonly called an IPO.

5.1 Phases of a Company's Life
Setting aside investment companies, the normal life-span of a company involves typical phases, shown below in tabular format for types one and two mentioned above.

	Group 1	Group 2
	Private Trading Companies Going Public	**Companies Formed for Public Quotation**
Private	Incorporate	Incorporate
	Start up	Acquire asset(s)
	*First income	
	Early growth	
Public	IPO (or placing)	IPO (or placing)
	Further growth	Acquire further assets
	Mature stage	Establish operations
	Acquisition/diversification(?)	*First income
	Conglomerate	Growth phase
	End of life	Mature stage
	Re-birth?	Acquisition/diversification(?)
		Conglomerate
		End of life
		Re-birth?

Table 5.1: Typical Phases of a Company's Life

The key difference, that can be seen from the table above, is that trading companies going public have their first income generation before going public and come to the market with a track record and usually have two or three years' of audited accounts behind them (different markets have different rules on this matter).

The second group, that starts trading after the IPO or placing, does not generate income until sometime after beginning its life as a public company. The money raised from the flotation is used to fund the establishment and/or development through to the income-generating phase. Sometimes there may be the need for further fund-raising to reach this stage.

This second group is much riskier than the first group, for the following reasons:

- No track record of trading
- Possible difficulties in reaching the point of income generation

(technical, political, under-estimation of start up costs, and inability to raise further funds).
- May not have suitable expertise (management, marketing, scientific, or technical) and/or may not be able to attract necessary skilled staff.

5.2 Going Out of Favour

Companies can go out of favour, and suffer a significant fall in share price, at any time and for a variety of reasons.

Over a number of years, I have observed several ways (and times) that this falling out of favour can happen, as follows:

- Post IPO (or placing)
- During early growth (growth glitch)
- Expansion problems
- Acquisition problems
- Diversification problems
- Sector cycles (e.g. commodity cycles)

Taking each theme in turn, common reasons for the change in company fortunes are summarised below.

Post IPO (and/or Placing)

For group 1 companies, the common thread seems to be that, at flotation or placing, the investor is being asked to pay too high a price for a share of the company. This seems, well to me anyway, to be evident, whatever the valuation method being used (PE, PSR, PBV, or PEG).

Also, expected growth levels often fail to materialize. Another book could be written on this subject but for now we'll just accept that, except in the most bullish of stock markets, it is unlikely that the share price growth will match the promotional hype of the IPO/placing documents.

With group 2 companies, reasons for poor share performance seem to be more to do with one or more of the following reasons:

- Technical challenges (especially for scientific and natural resource companies)
- Under-estimate of establishment or development costs (cash runs out)
- Dilution of shareholding (result of more shares being placed/sold)
- Investors get bored/tired of waiting

All of the above situations provide possibilities for the intelligent investor to pick winning shares, as we shall see at a later stage.

Early Growth Glitches

Any interruption to expected growth of a company, in its early stages, can dent the confidence of investors.

The reasons for the interruption (or glitch) can take many forms (technical, production problems, marketing issues, competition, external regulation, etc.). Frequently, the glitch may be of a temporary nature but the symptom is usually the same — a mark down of the share price.

Depending on how well the management cope with and resolve the issue(s) causing the glitch, recovery normally happens. Again, opportunity abounds for the DIY-Investor to pick winners from these casualties.

Expansion Problems

These can take many forms, according to the nature of the business/ industry that the company operates in. Common problems include:

- Retail companies not repeating their success in new locations
- Exploration/technical challenges (for oil, mining, chemical companies)
- Political or local cultural objections (where companies expand into different countries)
- Poor control of expansion costs
- Poor marketing and/or poor management

Using the techniques outlined later in this book, the intelligent DIY-Investor can succeed in picking winners that have suffered expansion problems.

Acquisition Problems

Problems arising from acquisition, where the target operates in the same sector as the buyer, can usually be traced to one or more of the following reasons:

- Over-paying for the acquisition
- Clashes in culture/management style
- Hidden financial problems within the company acquired
- Coincidental (external) changes affecting the market sector that the company occupies
- Poor integration/financial control of the enlarged operation
- Failure to exploit the opportunities (marketing, technological, scientific) arising from the acquisition

As before, the symptom is a declining share price. This can be over a short or medium time frame and is frequently not reversed without some changes in management.

Having resolved the issues, expansion can (usually) be recommended.

Diversification Problems

Diversification happens when companies invest their money into other types of business — often unrelated.

It is a trait that belongs to large, mature companies generating lots of cash. Forgoing opportunities to return cash to shareholders directly (via special dividends), or indirectly by buying back shares (increasing earnings per share for the reduced number of shares issued), the company diversifies.

Very few companies seem to manage this successfully. Some try, get poor results, and sell the offending company (frequently for less than they paid for it) and return to their stable mature phase.

Companies can operate as "cash-cows" in this state for many years (e.g. public utilities such as gas, water, telephones), providing solid cash returns to their shareholders by way of increasing dividends.

Opportunities for the DIY-Investor are more complicated to spot in this type of situation and so, for most of us, diversification is more likely to flag up forthcoming problems (rather than opportunities).

Sector Cycles

There are well established cycles and trends in economic life. I'm sure you will have noticed that very seldom do things remain constant. We always seem to be in boom or bust, inflation or deflation, high or low unemployment, high or low interest rates, high or low commodity prices, stable or unstable political and/or financial climates.

For the DIY-Investor looking to pick winning shares, it pays to be tuned in to these cycles. You might indentify a potential "winner" only to find that in the next year or two the whole sector falls flat on its face — leading to disappointing results.

Similarly, if interest rates are artificially low (as they are at the time of writing this book — autumn/winter 2010), then be aware of the affect that rising interest rates will have on companies that you are researching.

As we move on to consider strategies to pick winning shares, keep in mind the context of the life cycle of a company and look for shares that seem to be out of favour. In all of this do bear in mind that, for some companies, it's a one-way ride resulting in administration or receivership (going bust). You don't want to be holding the shares when this happens — believe me it's a painful experience.

6

STRATEGIES FOR PICKING
WINNING SHARES

When considering strategies for picking winning shares, many factors come into play. Fundamental to your choice of strategy must be an awareness of your characteristics and the amount of time you have to devote to picking and then managing your investments.

If, like me, you are passionate about managing your own finances and prepared to accept some risk in the quest for above-average rewards, then you need to devote a reasonable amount of time to get the desired results. Do not be fooled by those pundits trying to sell get-rich-quick courses for spectacular gains. The chances are that you will have paid £1500–£3000 for the privilege of two or three days of lectures, yielding some knowledge but not in sufficient depth to be of lasting benefit.

A better approach, in my opinion, is to seek your mentors through their writings. In particular, I recommend books by Graham & Dodds, Benjamin Graham, Peter Lynch, Jim Rogers, Jim Slater, Kenneth Fisher, and of course Warren Buffett (his annual reports to shareholders of Berkshire Hathaway are available on the internet free of charge). More details on recommended reading are given in appendix 2.

The amount of time that you can, or wish to, devote to being a DIY-Investor will affect whether you invest passively or actively.

6.1 Passive Investing

Passive investing for most people means choosing to buy index tracking funds, commodity funds, investment, or unit trusts. The common feature of all of these is that you are not buying shares in an individual trading company. The fund values do of course go up or down but not generally by a large percentage over a 12-month period.

They can be useful, even for an active investor, if you don't have an understanding of a particular sector, industry, or geographical region. You may wish to have a proportion of your money (say) in an investment trust in biotechnology companies. You may have insufficient specialist knowledge to analyse a company in this sector, but are of the opinion (from your general knowledge/awareness) that it is a growth area.

6.2 Active Investing

As the name suggests this involves some "doing." It involves research, analysis, selecting shares, buying your chosen shares, monitoring your investments, selling your shares (or some of them), re-investing, etc. For the DIY-Investor, it can be a rewarding passion that can provide you and your family with financial security and a degree of independence. Picking shares and managing your own self-invested pension plan (SIPP) is one area that I would urge all active UK investors to seriously consider.

Successful active investors frequently have several of the following attributes:

- Independence of thought
- A degree of contrarian thinking (going against the crowd)
- Have (or develop) specialist knowledge in a few investment sectors
- Some analytical abilities
- A wish to control their own finances
- Willingness to balance risk-vs.-reward (backing their own judgments)
- An ongoing desire to learn and improve their investment performance
- A reason to invest!

6.3 Buy Low — Sell High

It sounds very obvious but the essence of successful investing is to buy low and sell high. But what do "low" and "high" mean?

In real (£) terms, you need to sell your shares at a price higher than you bought them to make a profit. However, how do you decide what is a "low" price? Well, "low" can be judged by a variety of valuation measures, which we'll discuss in more detail later (see chapters 9 and 10).

Similarly, how "high" is high? Any investor will tell you of the many times when they have sold an investment only to watch the share price carry on up. So we'll also look at judging when to sell an investment (see chapter 15).

Over the past 15 years as a DIY-Investor, the strategy that has provided me with the greatest return has been to look for low-priced and/or depressed shares. These come in a variety of forms, which I have hinted at in chapter 5. Below, we'll look at my favourite four types.

6.4 Bruised "Big Un's"

These are major companies (usually in the FTSE 350) that are out of favour. The reasons for this can be:

- Through association with another company (in the same sector but performing badly)
- Missing an earnings target
- A downgrade or change of rating by an analyst
- The release of some "bad" news

The affect of this is to cause a significant fall in the share price, whether deserved or not. Falls of 30–70% are quite common and give rise to great opportunities for us DIY-Investors.

6.5 The Tide's Out!

When the whole stock market is going through troubled times, whether a medium or major correction, all companies seem to be affected. The banking crisis of 2008 to 2009 is the most notable recent example of this. In a major correction, there does not seem to be any discrimination between good, bad, or average companies, they are all like boats on the sea — all drifting lower as the tide of positive investment sentiment goes out. This creates, for DIY-Investors with cash to invest, good opportunities to buy great companies.

However, a word of caution to those who find themselves fully invested at the start of such a correction. You need to be aware of how you react emotionally under these conditions. It is very easy to get panicky and sell everything only to watch, in the following few days or weeks, the market recover all of its losses. Depending how long you have been invested, this can have the undesirable affect of leaving you out of pocket, having sold at a loss. Even worse, you may find that when your confidence does recover enough to re-enter the market, the share price is now higher than when you originally invested in the company.

6.6 Depressed Shares

The price of a depressed stock may well have dropped 75% or more from its high. To be truly depressed however, the share price must have been on a one-way downward slope over a timescale of two to three years (sometimes longer)!

Depressed stocks are frequently characterised by:

- No, or very little, broker coverage
- Lack of earnings forecasts
- Being out of favour (in the press and on bulletin boards)
- Being vilified by investors who bought them when they were highly priced (and who have lost most of their money as a result)
- No improvement, in share price, when there is good news reported (not believed?)

A good example of a depressed stock was GTL Resources (the AIM-listed ethanol producer, Epic: GTL). GTL joined AIM in September 2005 and through its American subsidiary, constructed a plant on the outskirts of Chicago to produce ethanol. The first part of the facilities opened in January 2007 and production was doubled to 100 million gallons per year when the plant was extended in 2008.

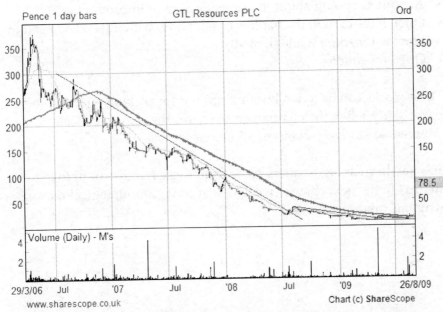

Fig. 6.1: GTL Resources (2006 to 2009) – A Very Depressed Stock

The share price (SP) graph illustrates very clearly the continuous decline in price. From the high of 377.5p (26th March 2006), GTL declined to 9p in April 2009 — a drop of 97.6% in the space of three years. The decline was in two distinct phases. From March 2006 to August 2008, the share price fell steeply and then the rate of decline reduced, producing a shallower pitch through to April 2009.

Now, you might be thinking "Were there any signs, for an alert DIY-Investor, in the gloom of the depressed GTL share-price performance in spring 2009?" Well, yes there were and we'll pick up the story of GTL in later chapters, as we look at the detail of how to pick winning shares.

6.7 Post-IPO Fallers

These are companies that have floated in the past year or two and often have many of the following attributes:

- Were issued at high valuations
- Subsequently disappointed their investors, usually by not matching the hype surrounding the IPO

- Are quietly going about their business, with improving results
- Often have cash in the bank, from the IPO, with little or no need to borrow for some while (if at all)
- Often forgotten

These stocks can be a rich hunting ground for picking winning shares, particularly when the company also shares the same characteristics as "depressed stocks," set out in 6.5 (above).

So why do such big winners come from these families of unloved shares? In the next chapter we'll look at some sound, logical reasons why this might be so.

7

THE REASONS BIG WINNERS COME FROM LOW PRICED/DEPRESSED STOCKS

7.1 Common Sense?

It is a well-recognised fact that the stock market overreacts at both the top and bottom of the market. This is true of the market as a whole and for us, more importantly, in the market for shares in individual companies and sectors.

In the market for individual shares, normal rules of supply and demand apply. If no one wants to buy the stock, the price declines and they become cheap. Similarly, for a "hot" stock, where everyone wants to own a slice of the action, demand outstrips supply and the price goes up.

For out-of-favour companies, it's not considered intelligent or sexy to own them. No one wants to admit to being bullish about their prospects. If you check on the bulletin boards, you'll find very little (if any) comment and what there is, is normally negative or downbeat. Similarly, there is usually very little news coverage in the financial press.

All of this adds to the right mix of conditions to create bargains for you, as an intelligent and independently-minded DIY-Investor.

7.2 Off the Radar Screen

Frequently, low priced and depressed stocks disappear "off the radar screen." This is true both for well-known "blue chip" companies and secondary companies (suffering from problems). However, the issue is even more noticeable for those companies lower down the pecking order.

When you search for out-of-favour companies, check for the following (typical) symptoms of unpopularity:

- Institutions have sold out (check the register of major shareholders online)
- No following by city analysts
- Few (if any) earnings forecasts available
- Poor write ups in financial magazines and/or newspapers (where you can find anything that is!)

The good news for DIY-Investors looking for bargains is that when a company's fortunes turn around or improve no one notices for a while. This gives us time to do our research and analysis and, if appropriate, to then invest. The essence of this approach is to be patient. It may take 12 months or more for the city, or other major investors, to start taking notice and the price to improve. Timing can be improved through the use of technical analysis (TA), as you will discover in chapter 8.

In some cases, when prospects start to improve for a depressed stock, there is an element of disbelief from professional analysts and fund managers who are reluctant to stick their necks out. This reluctance to go against the crowd seems to be due to the concern about the individual ranking of an analyst/fund manager amongst their peers. This may seem to be intuitively logical, given the normal human desire for job security, but gives us DIY-Investors a key advantage — no one's going to sack us.

7.3 Low Valuations & Low Priced – Why Do They Do Better?

It's worth restating the logical conclusion that if no one wants to own a company, then its shares will get marked down. When a low share price results, it's obvious that we can buy cheaply — the first essential part of finding winners. As many commentators have said "you make your profits when you buy," by which they mean buy low (cheap).

For low-priced shares, what may be overlooked is the fact that a rise of ¼p or ½p will be a big percentage rise. However, you need to be aware that, in so-called "penny shares" (those priced under £1), there will usually be a larger spread — the difference between the bid and offer price quoted by the stockbroker. Notwithstanding this note of caution, over a reasonable investment period of two to three years, gains of 100% or more can often be achieved.

Such investments, in low-valued and low-priced stocks, will generally be considered contrarian and/or "value" investments (they wouldn't be a popular choice). They are considered by the mainstream investor as being risky but with that risk comes the potential for greater reward. For long-term, index-beating performance, I'm happy to be considered both a contrarian and value investor.

7.4 What Can We Learn From Graham, Buffet, Lynch etc?

It would be very easy to write at length about such legendary investors. It would also be a source of great argument amongst investors as there are different "camps" that investors fall into.

My advice to you is to read widely to improve your financial education (in the context of investing). I believe in mentoring and through the writings of great investors (Benjamin Graham, Warren Buffet, Peter Lynch, Jim Rogers, Kenneth Fisher, etc.), there exists a great wealth of knowledge and experience that you can tap into. Some of my favourite books by my mentors are included in my suggestions for recommended reading (see appendix 2).

I have noticed common themes running through the writings and philosophies of great investors, including:

- A willingness to go against the crowd
- A desire to buy shares that represent value (i.e. are cheap based on one or more of the mentor's chosen measures)

- An analytical approach which considers pro's and con's for each potential investment
- Acknowledgement that they don't get it right every time (read Warren Buffet's annual letters to the shareholders of Berkshire Hathaway for candid acknowledgements on this front)
- Willingness to run winners and cut losers
- Awareness of wider issues (economic, technological, retail, fashion trends, etc.)

They are also great "teachers" — keen to pass on their knowledge to humanity through their writings.

From this chapter, you will have picked up the clear message that by any valuation measure you care to use, out-of-favour and depressed shares will be undervalued. To select these, the DIY-Investor will set the filtering criteria appropriately but how can we gain an edge to help us decide when to buy?

That's where technical analysis (TA) comes in...

8

USING SIMPLE TECHNICAL ANALYSIS

This chapter sets out some simple (but important) aspects of technical analysis that you can use to help decide when to buy, when to sell, and of equal importance when to continue to hold.

If you're looking for in-depth coverage of this topic, you're in the wrong place! See the recommended reading section in appendix 2 for my suggested books on this.

Technical analysis (TA) sounds very grand, for the subject of studying share price graphs. My preferred title is "wiggle watching" — which sounds much more fun!

8.1 Trends
Watch the TV news, read any financial magazine, glance in the business section of any national newspaper and you will quickly become aware that shares (and markets) are always moving up or down (or trending sideways).

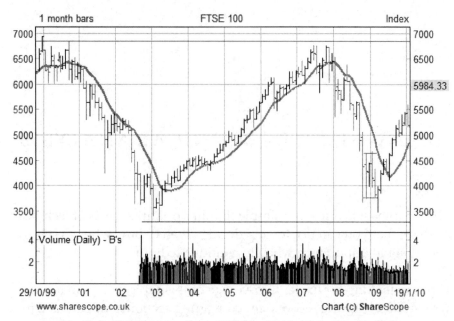

Fig. 8.1: FTSE 100 – from 2000 to 2010, Showing Trends

In the graph above, covering the FTSE 100 (index) over the past ten years, you can clearly see major, intermediate, and minor trends.

As prices move, you can draw lines between successive high points and successive low points to create trend lines. Patterns between trend lines also create shapes (wedges, flags, etc.). All of these have a place in TA and all can be applied over long, medium, or short timescales, sometimes referred to as major, intermediate, or minor trends (respectively).

When using TA, it always pays you to have a long- and short-term view of the price history. Downtrends, visible on the long-term view, may not be so obvious on the short-term view and once you have spotted this, it could prevent you from making a poor buying decision.

8.2 Moving Averages

To smooth out the effects of daily, weekly, or monthly price movements, it always pays to plot moving averages. These can be simple or exponential (which gives more weight to recent price movements).

My preference is to use the simple moving average (SMA). Choice of time frames is also personal but note that the 200-day SMA is often used in the financial press — and hence is widely observed.

My personal choices for SMA time periods are 10, 50, and 200 days. I also use the same choice — 10, 50, and 200 periods for analysing longer, weekly, or monthly time periods. My personal preference is to use OHLC (opening, high, low, close) bars — so that I can see the range (high-low) of the daily prices, as well as opening and closing price levels.

The smoothed out prices, represented by the 200-day SMA, conveys at a glance the general trend (up, down, or sideways). Observation of the changing trend in this, together with where the price is in relation to it, will play an important part in our analysis.

I sometimes feel that the 200-day SMA acts like a magnet, particularly if a rising share price creates a large "gap" between the price and its 200-day SMA.

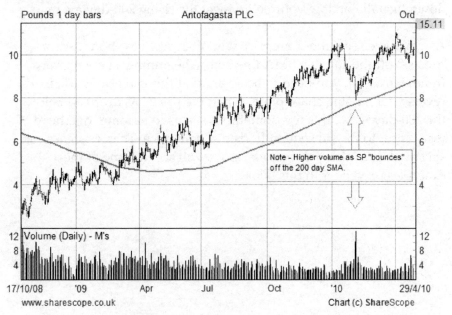

Fig. 8.2: Antofagasta – Moving Average (200 Day) as Support

53

As an example, consider the case of Antofagasta, the FTSE100 mining company (above). After more than a year climbing steadily upwards, in mid-January 2010, it began to fall back towards the 200-day SMA. However, over a period of four days (4th to 8th February 2010), it seemed to "bounce off" the 200-day SMA, on greatly increased volume. It then resumed its uptrend.

If you are a regular reader of the financial press, it would be easy to be sucked in by the hype and media attention surrounding the latest "hot stock." This can create a feeling that you should, or even must, invest to avoid losing out. You are probably feeling very confident that the share price will carry on rising.

However, you can see, from looking at the past (long-term) price action on any share price graph, that whenever the price moves too far from the 200-day SMA, they tend to be drawn back together again, as if by some form of magnetic attraction. This can happen by the share price entering a period of "lateral consolidation," allowing the 200-day SMA to "catch up." Alternatively, the price may drift back down (usually on low volume) to meet the rising 200-day average.

As you have seen, the shareprice will often seem to "bounce" (or reverse) off the 200-day SMA line before beginning a new upward trend. However, you need to be aware that this can also work, in reverse, for a rising share price. When the price has dropped below the 200-day SMA, this line sometimes seems to become "overhead resistance" to the subsequently rising share price. This resistance can stay in place for lengthy periods, as we will see in some of the examples used later in this book.

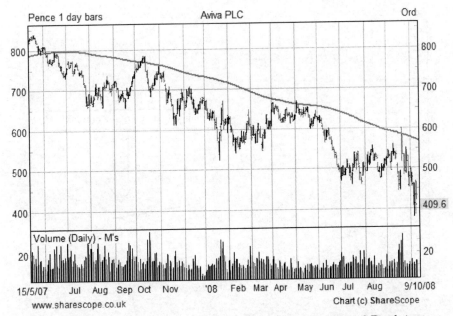

Fig. 8.3: Aviva – Moving Average (200-Day) as Overhead Resistance

Here, you can see that the insurance giant Aviva, having fallen through the 200-day SMA in spring 2007, continues on a downtrend for the next two years. During this time, the 200-day SMA acts as effective resistance to the rising share price.

8.3 Other Indicators

Volume

Volume of shares traded is one of the most useful supplementary indicators. Although it will be obvious that each trade has to match a buyer and a seller (the stockbroker usually being one or the other in each trade), it often adds weight to other indicators.

Significantly higher volume can act as a confirmation signal if a trend is broken or it can indicate an overbought or oversold situation at a change in trend (up to down or down to up).

Let's illustrate this with some examples.

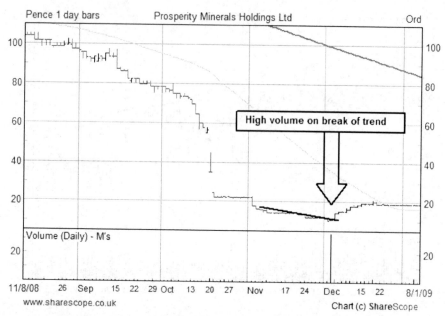

Fig. 8.4: Prosperity Mineral Holdings – High Volume at Bottom

Here you can see that, after a long period in decline, Prosperity Mineral Holdings (a Chinese cement manufacturer), bottoms out in early December 2008. This move broke the minor downtrend that had been in place for four to five weeks.

If you study the volume, plotted beneath the Sharescope graph, you can also see if a higher level of trading has been taking place, over a period of weeks. This can indicate increasing strength or increasing weakness, depending on other factors and indicators.

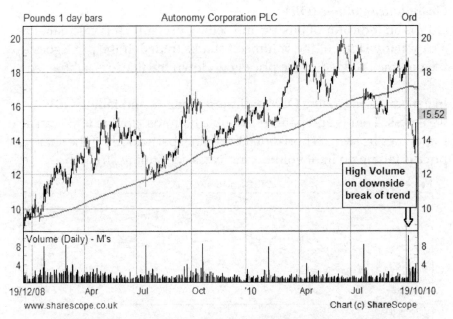

Fig. 8.5: Autonomy – High Volume on Breakdown of Trend

Similarly, volume can confirm a break of trend to the downside. You can see from the graph above, for the FTSE 100 company Autonomy, that following almost two years of a steady uptrend, the share price breaks down through the 200-day moving average in early October 2010. This marks a clear break of trend.

Relative Strength Indicator (RSI)

RSI is a momentum indicator which, in simple terms, indicates whether the share (or index or sector) is overbought or oversold. It is always expressed as a number between 0 and 100. Most people regard a reading below 30 as "oversold" and a reading above 70 as "overbought."

RSI can be simple, exponential, or the widely-used Wilder's RSI which smooths the reading. My preference is to use Wilder's RSI with the time period range (for smoothing) selected as 21 days.

The RSI line, normally plotted as an indicator below the graph, can be seen to follow trends and form its own patterns.

57

On-Balance Volume (OBV)

OBV is an indicator of buying and selling pressure. It is calculated as a cumulative total of the volume of shares traded. If the price goes up the volume is added, if the price goes down the figure is subtracted.

In general terms, rising OBV indicates strength, and falling OBV weakness. Trends and patterns (double bottoms, double tops) can also sometimes be seen. A horizontal OBV line, particularly if the share price is falling on light volume, indicates continuing strength.

Fig. 8.6: GTL Resources – Strong OBV Confirming "Hold" Stance

During the decline in GTL's share price (April to September 2010), I noticed that the OBV remained strong (level). As a result, I held my position, in anticipation of a resumption in the share price performance.

In my experience, a strong OBV is one of the most reliable supplementary indicators, where I'm looking for confirmation of my "hold" view on a share that I own.

Moving Average Convergence Divergence (MACD)

MACD is calculated from two exponential moving averages (EMA) of the share price. The result (long EMA subtracted from short EMA) being plotted against a signal, which is itself an EMA of the MACD reading. If that sounds confusing to you, join the club! However, all you need to know is how it works.

It is the crossing of the MACD over the signal line (either going up or going down) which provides the signal. The significance of the signal is dependant on the position of the crossover, coupled with the information available from the other indicators and the share price action.

MACD is important for revealing shifts in momentum and confirming trend direction. Like all indicators, MACD should be used in conjunction with other signals, price action, etc.

Stochastics
This is a complicated indicator, requiring daily high, low, and closing prices. In simple terms, without going into the mathematics behind the calculations, it reflects changing momentum. In practice, share prices (in a trend) normally slow down before they turn (up or down).

The indicator is indexed, staying between readings of 0 and 100. Signals are generated by crossovers of the stochastic indicator with its signal line, the significance of which depends on whether the indicator is overbought (above 70) or oversold (below 30).

As with most indicators, it is not advisable to use this on its own.

8.4 Turning Points (Up or Down)
Support and Resistance
This concept relates to the laws of supply and demand, as they affect the price of a share. Analysis of past share price action can generate clues as to the likely support and resistance levels.

Support is, as the name suggests, an apparent barrier to the share price dropping below a certain level. The more times a support level is tested, i.e. the share turns back up at the "support level," the stronger it is.

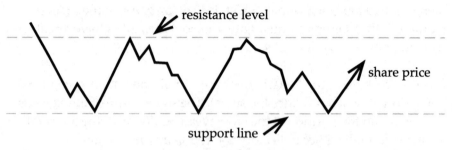

Fig. 8.7: Support and Resistance Levels

Conversely, resistance is the level that seems to provide an invisible barrier to a share price rising through it. The share price seems to bounce down from it. Again, the more times that this happens, the stronger the resistance. Let's have a look at an example of how support works in practice ...

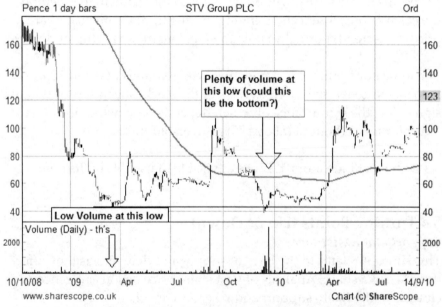

Fig. 8.8: STV Group – Volume at Turning Points

You can see from this example (above), that the FTSE fledgling company, Scottish TV Group, seemed to be "bottoming" from spring 2009 to spring 2010. There was support for the price about 43p. In mid-December 2009, you'll note that the price briefly dips below the 200-day SMA, only to be forced back up on strong volume. Later, during intra-day trading on 15th February 2010, the share price once again drops close to the support line, before closing the day at 47p.

You also need to be aware that lines of support or resistance can be horizontal or sloping. Previous turning points, going back over months or even several years, can often remain as significant support or resistance levels for the future.

As an example of a share price struggling to break up through a resistance level (or line), consider the case of Real Good Food Group (see Fig. 8.9 below).

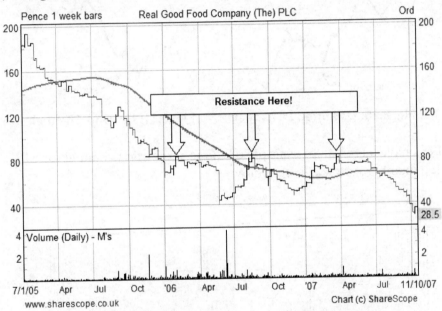

Fig. 8.9: Real Good Food – Overhead Resistance

You can see that from the beginning of 2006 through to spring 2007, the share price had three failed attempts to break through the price resistance level (at 82.5p). In the future, this resistance line will probably feature again, as future resistance, to any new price uptrend that may develop as the company's fortunes improve.

Using Sharescope, it pays to look back over the long-term price history and to mark significant support and resistance levels. As you mark them, use the "extend line forward" feature to make sure that you are aware of their existence as you monitor the price action in real time. In my experience, they will almost certainly have a future impact — acting (again) as either support or resistance.

Trend Lines

Long-term trend lines, being lines joining previous highs (for resistance) and previous lows (for support) can provide valuable clues for likely turning points when analyzing the zigs and zags of an individual stock price over the short term.

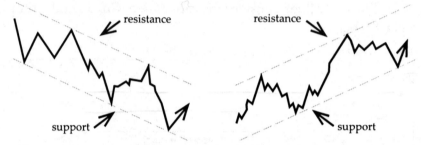

Fig. 8.10: Downtrend Channel   **Fig. 8.11: Uptrend Channel**

Let's have a look at an example of a long-term trend channel for FTSE 100 member AstraZenecca (below).

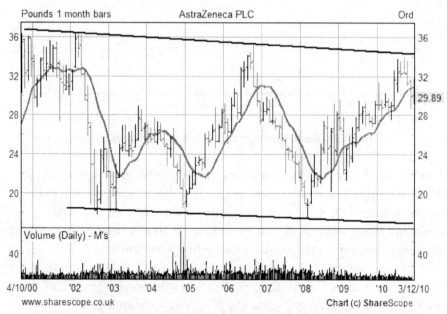

Fig. 8.12: AstraZenica – Long-Term Trend Channel

The importance of these long-term trend lines will be obvious to you, when considering the graph above. Can you imagine the disappointment if you had bought AstraZenica, at around £33, in autumn 2006 — not being aware that there was a long-term trend (resistance) line, going back several years? By the beginning of 2008, some fifteen months later, you would have seen the price almost halve to £18.

Moving Averages

Moving averages and crossovers of price with moving averages are frequently observed indicators of turning points (reversals) in established trends.

One of the most-watched crossovers is price crossing (up or down) through the 200-day moving average. As it is so widely observed, it pays to take note of such crossovers — particularly if reinforced by other indicators.

One variation of the moving average crossover is the "golden cross," another classic buy signal watched for at turning points. It occurs when a faster moving average (say 10 day) crosses up through a slower moving average (say 50 day). It follows that the share price is above the two moving averages that form the golden cross pattern.

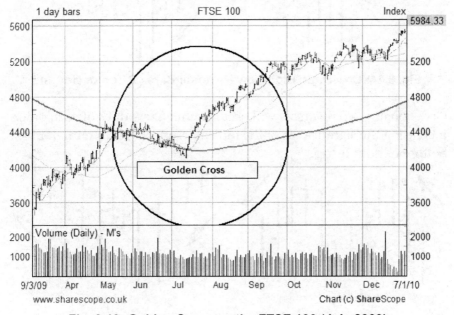

Fig. 8.13: Golden Cross on the FTSE 100 (July 2009)

63

You can see, from the example of the FTSE 100 index (previous page), that the "golden cross" was evident in mid-July 2009, as the 10-day SMA passed up through the 50-day SMA. This began an intermediate uptrend in the FTSE 100 that would last for the next nine months.

As you have seen, moving averages themselves, particularly the much-watched 200-day SMA, can act as a turning point for the share price. You might also have noticed that frequently, during an uptrend or downtrend, that the 50-day SMA can also act as support or resistance. These rules can be applied to any share, sector, or index.

Low-High/High-Low Reversal

One of the most important patterns to learn to identify is that of the low-high or high-low reversal. When confirmed by other indicators and the general shape of the price chart, it can provide timely indicators of turning points (buying or selling).

In simple terms such a reversal is indicated by two long bars with the closing prices being at opposite ends of the bar (see Fig. 8.14, below).

Fig. 8.14: Low-High, High-Low Reversal Bars (at Top or Bottom)

Occasionally two reversals will occur within a few days of each other increasing the significance of the indicator, effectively, a mini double bottom or double top.

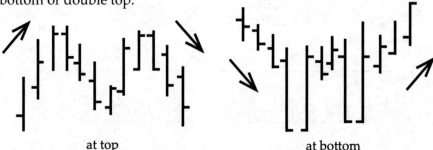

at top   at bottom

Fig. 8.15: Pairs of Reversal Bars (at Top or Bottom)

My own observations are that this type of reversal often consists of longer bars than those preceding or following (except where a double high-low happens). It is also a particularly strong indicator if supported by an increase in volume.

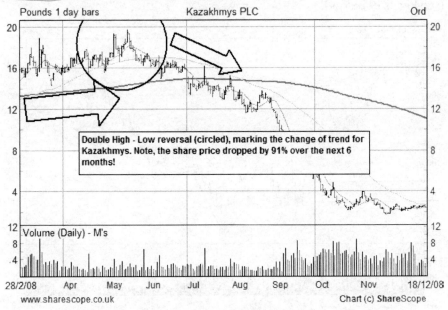

Fig. 8.16: Kazakhmys – Pair of High-Low Reversal Bars, Marking Change of Trend

8.5 Typical Patterns

Over time, certain patterns seem to repeat. A detailed study of the subject would warrant another book but in the context of our quest to pick winning shares, we'll pick out the (arguably) most significant ones.

Double Top/Double Bottom

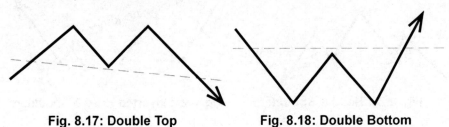

Fig. 8.17: Double Top   **Fig. 8.18: Double Bottom**

The double top/double bottom pattern is a frequently-observed pattern, occurring over weeks or even months. The pattern resembles an "M" shape (double top) and a "W" shape (double bottom) and the line marking the pattern (shown dotted above), can be horizontal or sloping (see Fig. 8.19 below).

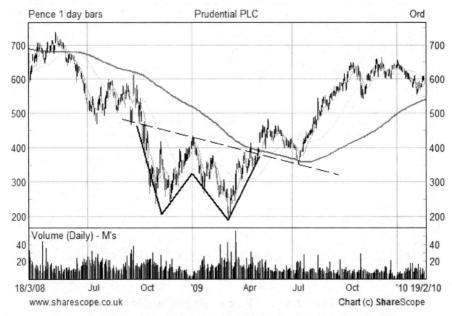

Fig. 8.19: Prudential – Double Bottom (Winter 2008–09)

Head & Shoulders

The head & shoulders is another classic pattern, occurring at a high-low turning point over a period of days, weeks, or even months. It can also take place with a horizontal or sloping "neck line." At a low-high turning point, the pattern is inverted.

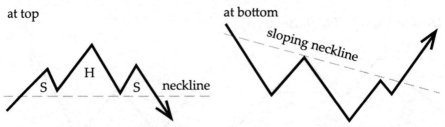

Fig. 8.20: Head & Shoulders   Fig. 8.21: Inverted Head & Shoulders

Where the "head" is not significantly above (or below, if inverted), the pattern may resemble a triple top/triple bottom. Both types of reversal patterns are considered by TA followers to be strong indicators of a reversal (see Fig. 8.22 below).

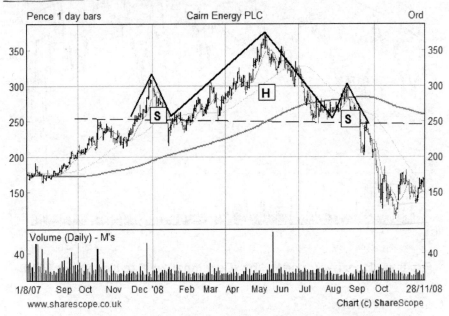

Fig. 8.22: Cairn Energy – Head & Shoulders Pattern
(Nov 2007 to Nov 2008)

Rounded Top/Bottom

The reversal of a company's share price can take place over a much longer timescale (possibly many months or years) and in a much more gentle way. Sometimes called a saucer top (or bottom), it is again considered to be a very strong reversal indicator.

Fig. 8.23 : Rounded Top   **Fig. 8.24: Rounded Bottom**

Bunzl, the FTSE 100 member, showed a good example of the typical "rounded top" pattern (see Fig. 8.25, on the following page). Note that this pattern took three years to unfold.

Fig. 8.25: Bunzl – Rounded Top (December 2005 to November 2008)

Triangles & Wedges

Triangles, usually characterized by one horizontal long side and one sloping long side, or wedges (truncated triangles), can occur at turning points and occasionally in mid trend.

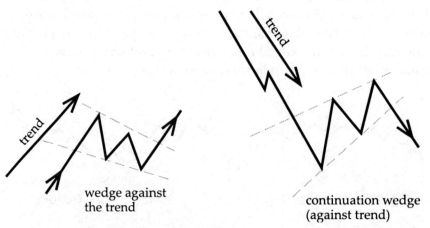

Fig. 8.26: Continuation Wedge (Against the Trend) – Up and Down

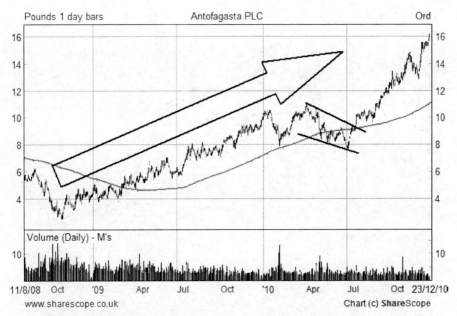

Fig. 8.27: Antofagasta – Continuation Wedge (Against the Trend)

Antofagasta (Fig. 8.27, above), illustrates nicely the continuation wedge pattern, which goes against the general upward trend. Whether you opt to sell or not will depend on how you view the long-term prospects of the company. Checking the fundamentals (PSR, PE, PEG, etc.) together with any recent news stories will help you to decide.

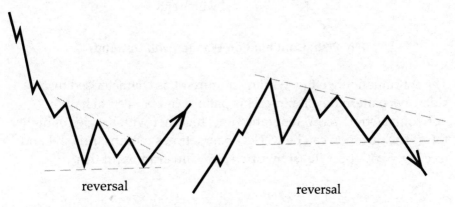

Fig. 8.28: Triangle (Wedge) at Reversal of Trend (Bottom and Top)

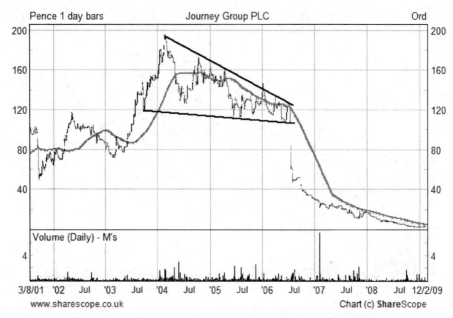

Fig. 8.29: Journey Group – Reversal Triangle at Top

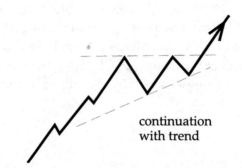

continuation
with trend

Fig. 8.30: Continuation Wedge (with Uptrend)

The continuation wedge, within an uptrend, is characterised by a sideways pattern developing. This pattern can be seen to have a horizontal (short-term) resistance line, together with a series of higher lows. The duration can be weeks or sometimes months. British Land (see Fig. 8.31, opposite) shows two clear illustrations of this.

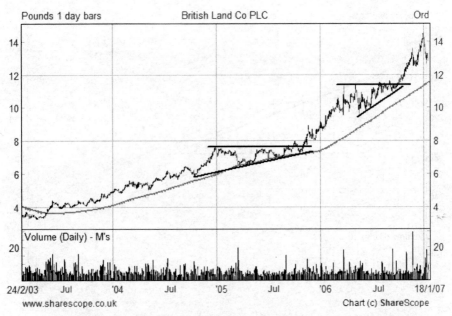

Fig. 8.31: British Land – Continuation Wedges (Within Uptrend)

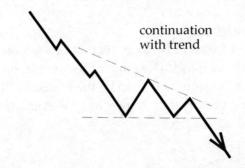

continuation
with trend

Fig. 8.32: Continuation Wedge (with Downtrend)

This opposite pattern will frequently occur during a long-term downtrend. Care must be taken here, for if you believe that the horizontal (support) line is the "bottom" of the decline, you may buy too early. This is well illustrated in the case of Haike Chemicals (see Fig. 8.33, on the following page).

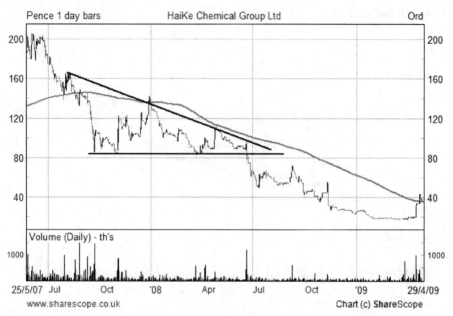

Fig. 8.33: Haike Chemicals – Continuation Wedge (Within Downtrend)

8.6 Lateral Breakouts

One of the quietest forms of breakout is that of a lateral (sideways) breakout from a downtrend. The longer the downtrend (e.g. two or three years), the more significant can be the breakout. If spotted, it also gives a golden opportunity to buy at a low valuation.

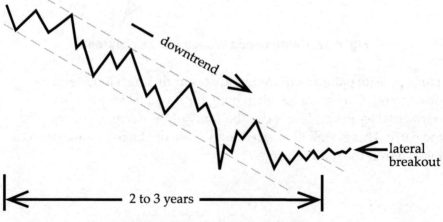

Fig. 8.34: Typical Lateral Breakout

You will see that these lateral breakouts are frequently followed by a bullish zig-zag being a rise, followed by a higher low, then a new higher high (in the short-term trend).

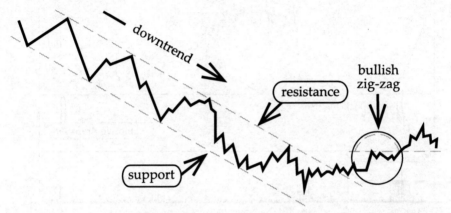

lateral breakout with bullish zig-zag

Fig. 8.35: Typical Bullish Zig-Zag, Following Lateral Breakout

Also typical of these lateral breakouts is the pullback (or drifting back) to a line of support. This support can be at the price level of the lateral breakout or the level of the first pullback within the first bullish zig-zag. What is also typical is the increased volume marking the change in trend (minor trend reversal) that precedes the pullback or drift back down to support.

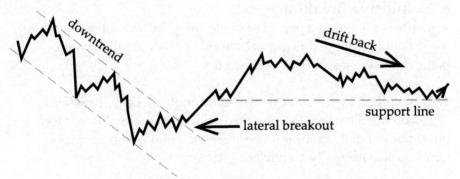

lateral breakout with "drift back" to support line

Fig. 8.36: Typical "Drift Back," Following Lateral Breakout and Rise

Fig. 8.37: Sunkar Resources – Lateral Breakout, Rise, and "Drift Back"

The above graph shows Sunkar Resources, an AIM-listed phosphate fertiliser manufacturer. You can see quite clearly that the share price "drifted back" from its high (46.5p) on 9th October 2009 to find support at 17p at the end of July 2010. The downtrend was broken by another "explosive breakout" at the beginning of September 2010.

8.7 Explosive Breakouts

Sometimes following a period of "bottoming" after a lateral breakout, triple bottom, rounded (saucer) bottom, or other similar basing pattern, an "explosive breakout" occurs.

This is typified by the price breaking through a level of resistance, coupled with significantly increased volume (usually three or four times normal daily volume). The size of the move, in percentage terms, is also normally significant (>10%).

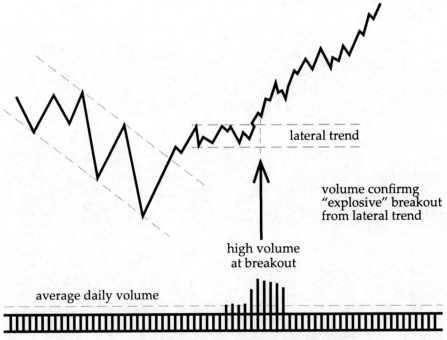

Fig. 8.38: Typical "Explosive Breakout"

Once breached in such a fashion, the old level of resistance frequently becomes the new level of support on any subsequent pull back. You can see, in the example of Sunkar Resources (Fig. 8.37, opposite), that the price more than doubled on the first explosive breakout (late September 2009) and almost doubled in the second breakout at the beginning of September 2010.

More often than not, an explosive breakout marks the beginning of a new major (or at least intermediate) uptrend.

8.8 Summary of Simple Technical Analysis

You will have seen, from the examples that I have included, that the patterns are never (or rarely are) perfect. Nevertheless, they repeat often enough to be of significant use, when "wiggle watching."

Now that you have the basic TA tools under your belt in the quest to pick winners, let's move on to pick out the key parts of fundamental analysis for you.

9

HOW TO USE KEY ASPECTS OF
FUNDAMENTAL ANALYSIS

9.1 It's all in the numbers!

Fundamental analysis is all about numbers. It relies on analysis of what we know about the performance of a company, based on its business and accounts. Projections of the future prospects for the company are also a key part of fundamental investing.

Analysis of the past can be done manually by the DIY-Investor but we can make better use of our time by using any one of a number of on-line sources for historical analysis. Nearly all on-line stockbrokers also provide this information free of charge.

Projections of future prospects, generally involving profit and earnings per share (EPS) forecasts, are a little more tricky. Fortunately, the same free sources of on-line historical data will contain a summary of the consensus forecasts. These are prepared by professional analysts and the larger and more popular a company is, the more analysts follow it.

My approach to picking winning shares relies on a combination of analysing the following:

• A few simple balance sheet ratios (and trends)
• Turnover and profit analysis
• Earnings and PE ratios (historical, sector, and market)
• Cash flow generation (current and historical)

Let's look at a few of these in more detail....

9.2 Balance Sheet

The balance sheet is a snapshot of a company's position at a given point in time. In the UK we get two of these a year, one with the interim (six-month) results and one at the end of the company's financial year. In the USA this information is provided quarterly.

For any serious devotee of value investing, the balance sheet is critical. For our needs, as DIY-Investors, we want to pick out the following points:

- Level of debt (both short term and long term)
- Cash and cash equivalents (listed under current assets)
- Book value (the difference between total assets and total liabilities)
- Tangible book value (total book value less intangible assets)
- Trends in the above (some companies put a table in the notes to their annual accounts giving the five-year record)

Key ratios link balance sheet figures to the current price of the company, either on a per-share basis or for the whole company (the ratios are the same). Fortunately for us, as DIY-Investors, most of this is available on-line for free.

Book Value

Book value can hide nasty surprises or conversely conceal hidden gems. Nasty surprises can come in many forms: overvalued inventory (particularly in clothes retail or technology companies), machinery that is obsolete, real estate under construction (possibly overvalued), work in progress that doesn't materialize (service companies).

On the other hand, careful analysis can reveal hidden gems in assets that in reality don't depreciate. They may have been written down to negligible worth in a company's accounts or the gems can be investments valued at cost (concealing their true increased worth). Brand names can also have significant worth (Disney and Coca-Cola spring to mind).

From a DIY-Investor's point of view and in order to pick winners, the following table sets out my suggested criteria (for purchase):

		Excellent	Good	Cut-Off
Price/book value	PBV	<0.5	0.75	1.5
Price/tangible book value	PTBV	<0.3	0.5	1.0
Net gearing		<25%	50-75%	100%

These ratios work for me but, as with all aspects of DIY-investing, you need to make up your own mind. The whole essence of this book is to encourage you to do just that.

Cash
Cash and cash equivalents are, or should be, based on solid fact. The trend between a series of three or four balance sheets should (ideally) reveal an improving cash situation. The only caveat to this statement is that, if a large disposal has been made by a company, the cash position may have been artificially (and perhaps temporarily) inflated. Careful analysis of the company's accounts on an "ongoing basis" may be necessary to confirm value.

Debt
Similarly, a company getting stronger will reduce its debt, unless it expands. The structure of a company's debt is also very important. Short-term debt can be recalled (as seen in the recent banking crisis) and can cripple a business. Long-term (funded) debt, repayable in a few years time, provides the lifeblood of most businesses.

These last two points can be summed up as:

- Increasing cash is good
- Increasing debt (particularly short-term) is, or can be, bad

9.3 Turnover and PSR
Turnover (sales) is the top line of a profit and loss account and yet is sometimes almost ignored by the popular financial press.

The historic price-to-sales ratio (PSR) can be calculated for the whole company, by dividing the MCAP (market capitalisation) by the total sales from the last annual accounts. A figure below 1.0 is good and a figure below 0.5 deserves a much closer inspection. However, you need to be aware of sector differences. In general terms, sectors with high turnover and low profit margins (e.g. food retailers) have relatively low PSR's. The opposite is true for sectors where high profit margins are the norm (e.g. technology).

Where a share is depressed or out of favour, knowledge of the highest and lowest PSR figures for each of the past three or four years can provide an insight to future ratios (and hence prices) that can be expected when turnaround or recovery happens.

Similarly, comparison of the current company PSR, with that of its sector and the market as a whole, can give a feeling of whether a company is undervalued or not. The current PSR can be considered a measure of the "popularity" of the company by investors.

When a company has a low PSR and undergoes a change in fortune, or is perceived as being in a "turnaround" situation, it often becomes more popular and is re-rated. This re-rating, measured by increasing PSR, has a multiplying affect on the share price (see below):

	Company A	Company B
Share price	64p	27p
Turnover per share	£4.00	£4.00
PSR	0.16	0.08
Growth in turnover	+10%	+10%
Future turnover per share	£4.40	£4.40
New PSR	0.16 (static)	0.12 (+50%)
New share price	70.4p	52.8p
Price % increase	+10%	+95.5%

In the example above, you will note that both companies have increased their turnover by 10%. The PSR for company "A" has remained static and the price has therefore only appreciated by 10%. For company "B," where the popularity is increasing, the PSR ratio has increased by 50% (to 0.12). The multiplication affect of this, coupled with the increase in turnover, improves the price by 95.5%.

80

This type of PSR analysis is particularly useful when assessing possible turnaround candidates, where the company has suffered a loss, and therefore has no earnings (or PE ratio). A cursory assessment of the trend in turnover (growing, flat, or reducing), coupled with PSR analysis, can prove to be very rewarding. We will look at this in more detail in the case studies contained in chapter 16.

9.4 Profit

Some people get confused between gross profit, net profit, EBIT, EBITDA, and earnings per share (EPS).

Gross profit is the sales (or turnover) from the trading activity less the direct costs required to produce the turnover. For example, taking the example of a publisher, turnover would normally come from sales of newspapers, magazines, etc. plus advertising income, less the direct costs of the staff, newsprint, etc. used in the publishing processes.

Net profit on the other hand comes from taking the fixed costs (premises costs, business rates, insurances, accountancy costs, etc.) away from the gross profit.

This net profit will be before tax (termed PBT) and net profit after tax is what is left for the company to distribute (as dividends), re-invest in expansion/modernisation, or possibly to invest in another business.

Where this investment is in the same type of business, it is quite simply expansion of the business. However, some businesses diversify into other (non-related) businesses and this is not always so successful. Peter Lynch (in his superb book *One up on Wall Street*) terms this "diworseification" and with good reason. Historically, profitable companies seem to have a habit of over-paying for acquisitions and frequently fail to get the same profitable returns from these purchases. Such diversification activities are, in my opinion, a negative sign.

However, you need to be aware that some of the costs included in the accounts are "non-cash costs." These include depreciation and amortisation.

Depreciation is the writing off (or writing down) of capital cost items such as machinery, plant & equipment, etc. For example if an open cast mining company invests in excavators and lorries/dumper trucks costing £2 million, it will normally depreciate this investment by 25% each year (including £500,000 in the first years accounts).

If a company expands by buying another business, paying above the book value of that business, then this "goodwill" is an intangible value and the writing off is termed amortisation. The notes to the accounts set out the company's policy on amortisation but note that directors have more freedom to write down values. Writing down is particularly noticeable when a company is going through a tough time and the share price is being hammered. Directors often use this as an excuse to write off all manner of costs in an attempt to get all the bad news out of the way, prior to resumption of growth. Similarly, directors can "accrue" for an anticipated cost, which then reduces stated profits.

As DIY-Investors, we need to look at the trend of profits (usually PBT or operating profit). This is particularly important when we're looking at turnaround opportunities or bruised blue chip (or other secondary companies) that have had a temporary setback.

Short-term "losses," particularly following write offs, are often penalised. For the DIY-Investor who takes the trouble to look below the surface, great opportunities can be found.

9.5 Earnings and Price to Earnings (PE)

The profit, after tax and interest charges, is the "reward" (or earnings) for the shareholders. The total earnings, divided by the number of shares, provides the earnings per share (EPS) — a much-touted figure. Dividing the price per share by the earnings per share gives us the PE ratio — one of the most publicised valuation measures of a company, so beloved by city analysts and the financial press.

Interpretation of this PE figure can be done by cross-referencing to one or more of the following:

- Other similar companies (in the same sector)
- The whole stock market
- The company's historical PE ratios (high and low values for the past five years)

If you decide that a particular sector is worth investing in, comparison of possible investment opportunities should include the PE comparison within the peer group.

For the DIY-Investor, PE is a useful measure — particularly when combined with other valuation techniques.

9.6 Cash Flow and Price-to-Cash Flow (PCF)

The cash-flow statement is the third in the statutory financial statements of a publicly-listed company, normally following immediately behind the P&L and balance sheet.

It takes the cash flow from operating activities and adjusts it for the non-cash costs, referred to above, together with a whole series of adjustments including:

- Asset impairment and/or reversal
- Profits on disposals (businesses, machinery, etc.)
- Adjustments to pension fund contributions
- Interest paid (and received)
- Capital purchases (land, machinery, businesses)
- Financing activity – cash flow in or out of the business
- Decrease/increase in inventory
- Dividends paid
- Share options exercised
- Foreign exchange adjustments
- Increase/decrease in working capital
- Increase or decrease in "provisions"

At the end of the statement the net "cash and cash equivalents" is shown for the end of the accounting period (i.e. the balance sheet date).

The cash flow will usually show the following:

- Cash utilised by/generated from operations
- Net cash (after interest and tax adjustments) utilised by/generated from operations
- Net cash outflow/inflow from investing activities
- Net cash inflow/outflow from financing activities

It is these figures added/subtracted which lead to the net decrease/increase in cash and cash equivalents. This is a key figure! It can provide clues to show whether the company is generating and retaining more cash than it needs to operate. Of equal importance, it shows what the company is doing with this cash.

Cross references to the notes in the accounts are particularly useful, as are the comparisons for the prior (equivalent) accounting period.

The statement also shows how this figure is split between cash at bank (and in hand), together with bank overdrafts. You will remember that short-term debt can be recalled and, not surprisingly, too much of this is generally considered bad.

Dividing the net cash inflow/outflow by the number of shares gives the cash flow per share.

For the DIY-Investor, one of the key checks is to make sure that the net cash flow (per share) is not less than the EPS figure. For good cash-generating businesses, it is normally higher.

Companies that have to re-invest heavily just to maintain their current level of business (e.g. steelworks) can be risky investments as there may be little "free cash" to expand the business or pay dividends.

Price-to-Cash Flow (PCF)

If a share, priced at £2, has net cash flow of 20p/share, then its PCF = 10. This would be considered by most to be standard. In effect your investment of £2 in the company is yielding, for the company, a 10% return in cash. A PCF of 5 or less is very good and a PCF of 2 or less, providing it's not negative, represents an exceptional find.

For the DIY-Investor this ratio, like most balance sheet (snapshot) ratios, should be checked against:

- The trend in the company's PCF ratios
- PCF's for the peer group (sector)
- PCF's for the market as a whole

9.7 Summary of Simple Fundamental Analysis

There is a vast array of facts and figures available to the DIY-Investor looking to select shares that will become winners. Of these, the six key numbers for me (shown with their cut-off threshold, good and excellent ratings) are:

	Excellent	Good	Cut-Off
PSR	< 0.5	0.5–1.0	1.5
Net gearing	< 25%	25%–75%	100%
PTBV	< 0.3	0.3–0.75	1.0
PCF	< 2	2–5	10
PBV	< 0.5	0.5–1.0	1.5
PE	< 5	5–10	15

It is highly unlikely that, using the above criteria as filters, any company will match all of them. If you are considering a share and, on the above criteria, it does match everything and looks too good to be true, watch out, it probably is!

However, if when looking at the figures for any share that passes through your chosen set of filters into your basket of "possibles," check for violation of the cut-off threshold for the other ratios (not used as filters). Unless this can be justified, following further investigation, put a black mark against it in your analysis.

The use of fundamental analysis techniques, by themselves, to pick winning shares has some drawbacks. In particular, an individual company may meet DIY-Investors criteria as a good (or even excellent) share to purchase and yet the price may go nowhere (or worse still significantly decline) after purchase. How can we reduce the chances of this happening and increase the chances of picking winners?

The answer lies in the next chapter… by combining technical and fundamental analysis to pick winning shares.

10

HOW TO BLEND TECHNICAL AND FUNDAMENTAL ANALYSIS TO PICK WINNING SHARES

10.1 Searching for Winners

I almost called the sub-title of this book "How to find big profits among the bruised, battered, or depressed stocks that nobody wants." Although I decided it was a bit of a mouthful, the essence of what I was getting at, is…

Big winners come from out-of-favour stocks!

You will have picked up, from chapter 7, the essential point about a stock being out of favour is that its share price (SP) is low or even very low. We, as intelligent DIY-Investors, aim to buy low and sell high, it's as simple as that. However, this does throw up some interesting questions, when searching for winners, including:

- How low is low?
- Is the share price likely to go lower?
- How do we know the company won't go bust?
- When should we buy it?
- How long should we hold it?
- When should we sell it?
- How high should the SP get before we sell it?

My personal strategy is to look for capital growth and so, for me, dividends are a bonus. However, in a few years time as I start to think about retirement, at least from my day job, I will start to pay more interest in dividends from my investments.

So why am I suggesting the focus on low priced and/or depressed stocks? The answer lies in my belief, based on my fifteen years of investing, in the following benefits:

- Reduction in risk (undervalued shares are normally less susceptible to market downturns)
- Greater returns (annual growth rates of 20% + should be achievable)
- Greater proportion of "doublers" (shares that double in value within 2–3 years)
- "Ten baggers" are a possibility (shares that increase tenfold over a period of 2–5 years)

As DIY-Investors, I believe we need a degree of contrarian thinking. What good is it to follow the herd? The likely outcome is that, in doing so, you'll follow the market. Our aim is to outperform the market.

10.2 How to... My DIY-Investors Way!

In summary, my way is to combine fundamental and technical analysis to filter (select) from the whole market to create a watch list. From the watch list, I select shares to purchase, assuming that I have funds sitting in cash.

I monitor the shares regularly, normally daily.

If a company's prospects change (for the worse) and/or I consider it overvalued, I sell the shares (or part of the holding).

There are all sorts of twists and turns to this strategy but the overall approach is shown in the diagram opposite.

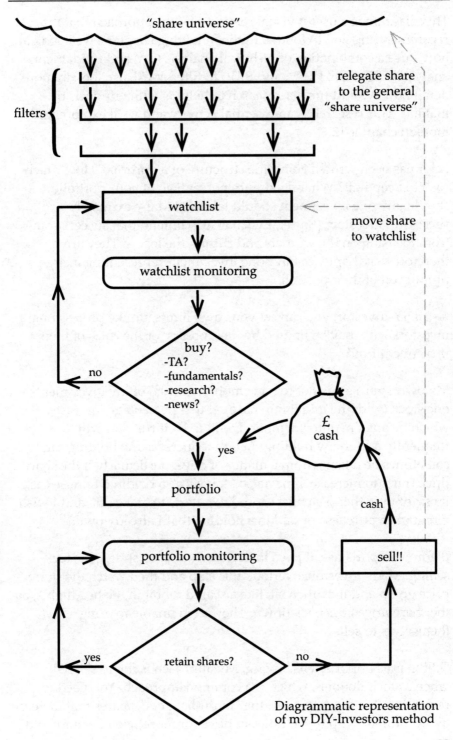

Diagrammatic representation
of my DIY-Investors method

This diagram is a useful visual reminder of the approach that I'm recommending you to follow. In the following chapters, we'll look at how I use a combination of technical analysis (TA) and fundamental analysis (PSR, PCF, PTBV, and PBV) to filter. We'll also look in more detail how we add further research to help us with our decision making. This research is an essential activity and we'll explore this more in chapter 12.

A lot has been written about the structure of a portfolio. How much cash to keep in it? What maximum percentage of your portfolio should any one investment should take up? Many extremely successful investors (Buffet, Lynch et al.) contend that success comes from focusing on the winners and cutting the losers. They are therefore very happy to have one investment representing a large proportion of their portfolio.

As a DIY-Investor, you can set your own limits, unlike professional investors who may be limited by their bosses, or the rules of their investment fund.

My own approach is not to have more than 10% of my investments in one stock (with the initial purchase). If that percentage increases — which means I'm onto a winner, I tend to let it run and will frequently add to my holding. Action to increase my holding can sometimes be taken within a matter of days, particularly if the share price starts to increase. I may also "top slice" a holding, to raise cash, if one of my other watchlist candidates starts to "take off" and I wish to initiate a purchase or add to a holding that I already own.

Before you purchase, it pays to decide what your strategy is for selling. Many investors overlook this step and then watch the share price go up and they then sit, like a scared rabbit in the headlights, as the share price goes back down. They seem unable to bring themselves to sell.

Selling is as important as buying. My approach is not to sell half when a stock doubles, which is a common approach. You need to remember that if you are seeking "multi-baggers", shares that increase by two, three — up to ten times in price (or more), you need to hold on past this point. Instead, I prefer to sell part (or all) of a holding when it is overvalued, or if there is some bad news. We'll look at this in more detail in chapter 15.

Let's break this process down into easily-digested chunks. In the next chapter, we'll take a closer look at the first part of picking winning shares — how to filter from the universe of shares to create a watchlist.

11

FILTERING TO CREATE YOUR "WATCHLIST"

With such a vast universe of shares available to you, you are probably thinking "where do I start?" This chapter covers the essential first step of my strategy for picking winning shares, with the aim of creating a manageable basket of shares that you can "keep tabs on" with a view to making a purchase.

The "how to" part of this book would be tedious, if not almost impossible, if computers didn't exist. My personal choice for selection and monitoring is "Sharescope," a versatile program that runs on any PC. I use "Sharescope Gold," which utilizes end-of-day stock price downloads via an internet connection. We'll look at this in a bit more detail below.

11.1 Initial Selection (from Market to Watchlist)
Having loaded the main Sharescope table, take the following steps:

1. Set up a portfolio and label it appropriately (say "watchlist")

2. Using the data mining function (pick & shovel button on the top bar), we select the following three criteria:

- Price between two dates (two years ago compared to today's date). Set between -98.00 and -50.00 (this yields shares that have fallen between 50 and 98% over the past two years). For a share to be "bruised, battered, or depressed" it must be down by at least 50%. You may decide to select down by -75% as the (higher) cut-off when you select the filter, to reduce the number of selections.

- Turnover/Cap set to above 2.0 (and below 40 if you want to eliminate any rogue outsiders). On Sharescope, Turnover/Cap is the PSR formula inverted, i.e. total sales divided by MCAP. Thus to get a PSR of 0.5 (or below), you need to select Turnover/Cap. above 2.0. The higher the Turnover/Cap figure, the lower the PSR.

- MCAP between £5 million and £500 million. In terms of looking at size of company, this third selection criteria — MCAP between £5 million (lowest level) and £500 million (highest level) — is my starting point. The highest level on this filter brings a good chance of scooping up some "bruised" blue-chip companies. I normally have this criteria set as the "z" axis, which provides a larger plotted square representing the bigger companies.

Using the data mining facility of Sharescope and the above three criteria yields a display like this...

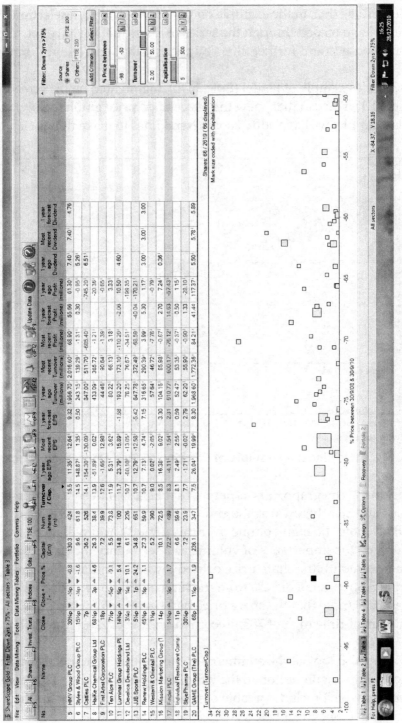

Fig. 11.1: Sharescope – Data Mining Screen

You will see that, in the example on the previous page, a selection of 66 shares have passed through the series of filters that we have set. You may choose to add further filters by clicking the "add criteria" button.

Using the example of Findel (Epic: FDL), highlighted on the screenshot (Fig. 11.1), you can then view the Sharescope price graph (below). In this example, we have added some trend lines to make things clearer.

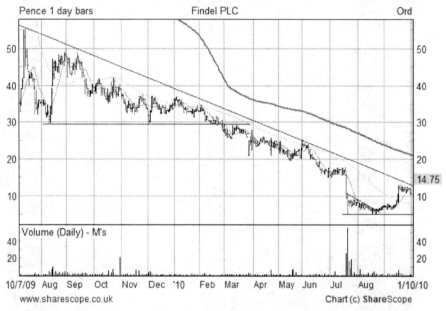

Fig. 11.2: Findel – Example of Filtering to Find Depressed Stocks

Looking at the graph, it is apparent that FDL is indeed a depressed stock and clearly towards the end of July 2010, there was a massive sell off (note the high volume over this period). You will recall from chapter 8 the importance of volume as a secondary indicator. Over the next month the share price drifted lower, eventually bottoming out at 5.6p — a fall of 96% from the high of 153.5p recorded on 13th May 2009 (note that the share price had been even higher in 2007, with an all-time high of 783p recorded on 21st & 22nd May 2007).

You can also look at the summary of the company financial details, by clicking the menu button to the left of the graph symbol. This reveals a screen which includes a table of recent financial history for the company (see extract below).

Key metrics	31/3/06 IFRS	31/3/07 IFRS	31/3/08 IFRS	3/4/09 IFRS	2/4/10 IFRS	1/3/11 Forecast
ROCE	20.77	20.23	18.90	5.02	11.89	
EPS (p)	35.26	32.04	35.28	-4.11	1.54	2.31
Turnover (£m)	527.80	596.78	645.06	610.77	600.17	542.89
Turnover ps (£)	4.27	4.72	5.19	4.90	1.59	
Dividend (p)	12.14	13.36	14.98	0.00	0.00	
Dividend yield	2.17	1.92	3.03			
Depreciation (£m)	7.84	10.02	6.39	11.72	13.46	
Net borrow (£m)	262.47	315.58	386.74	376.10	309.60	
Interest paid (£m)	14.70	17.37	21.78	22.58	19.20	
Interest cover	4.21	3.45	3.06	0.44	1.29	
Tax paid (£m)	4.93	1.39	8.46	-10.40	-0.57	
Operating margin	11.91	10.80	12.03	0.75	4.81	
Profit (£m)	35.07	18.39	25.16	-57.43	-76.12	14.63
ROE	34.23	29.48	36.74	-27.17	12.62	
Norm EPS (p)	35.26	32.04	35.28	-4.11	1.54	
FRS3 EPS (p)	23.67	12.03	13.22	-33.36	-20.02	
Cash flow ps (p)	-5.44	14.65	-12.91	31.86	2.73	
Net cash ps (p)	1.81	6.05	10.12	7.86	9.06	
Capex ps (p)	12.18	10.64	6.22	9.82	2.24	
R&D ps (p)	0.00	0.00	0.00	0.00	0.00	
Quick ratio	2.35	1.91	1.63	1.70	0.58	
Current ratio	3.36	2.67	2.25	2.22	0.74	
Net gearing inc.	215.11	259.27	348.40	1,163.89	922.12	
Gross gearing inc. (%)	216.98	265.54	359.90	1,194.61	1,054.14	
Gross gearing ex. (%)	680.21	-1,444.21	-989.33	-386.20	-418.91	
Gross gear. <1y inc (%)	16.06	27.55	60.09	134.92	1,054.14	
Tang. book value (£m)	38.93	-22.38	-40.38	-99.95	-84.49	
Book value (£m)	122.03	121.71	110.99	32.31	33.58	

Fig. 11.3: Findel – Financial Summary (from Sharescope)

From this Sharescope financial summary, you can see that Findel is a company that still has a significant turnover but is saddled with a high level of debt. However, its SP action suggests that it is bottoming and so you might decide to add it to your watchlist.

When I am doing this filtering/screening exercise, I normally also have my internet browser open, logged into my on-line broker (TD Waterhouse). Here, I'll use the research facilities to check other selection criteria, to help me decide whether to add Findel, or any other company that passes through my filters, onto my watchlist.

11.2 Fine Tuning (Using Other Criteria)

As in the example above, it's quite likely that by using the three criteria outlined above, you will have a large list of possible candidates (66 in our example). Using a combination of Sharescope (company details summary) and the company facts sheets from TD Waterhouse, I check the following criteria:

- PTBV – is it below 0.75?
- PE – is it low (relative to sector and market)?
- Net gearing % (below 100%?)
- EPS – how much (p/share) and how does this compare to historical and projected levels?
- PEG – the PEG (price-to-earnings growth) ratio
- Any directors dealings (buys/sells)?

How many you end up with on your watchlist is your choice, depending on the parameters that you set.

11.3 What to Choose?

This can be a difficult question to answer and is very much a matter of personal taste. Amongst the many choices you have to make are:

- What sector(s) to invest in (mining, media, retail, services, etc.)
- What geographical areas of operation (UK, Europe, Asia, Worldwide etc.)?
- Which stock exchange (London, FTSE, or AIM and/or foreign exchanges)?
- At the time of writing (autumn/winter 2010), my choices are based around the following (personal) observations:
  - Interest rates are at historically low levels, in the UK and elsewhere. I'm therefore very wary of companies with high gearing, where they may be adversely affected if interest rates rise.
  - As we come out of the global recession, it seems that the main geographical drivers for growth will be China, India, Africa and South America.
  - Growth, particularly in China and India (due to the size of their populations), will require vast quantities of commodities (coal, iron ore, heavy metals, etc.), together with an ever-increasing demand for energy.
  - Cyclical industries, badly hit by the recession, will come back to prosperity over the next few years.
  - Media and publishing companies are likely to stage a revival as the world economy improves and advertising revenues increase (they will however need to fully embrace digital and internet technologies to gain the full benefits).

Although I can't attach meaningful numbers to the above observations, in terms of setting selection criteria, I do keep them in mind as I go through the search and selection process.

Having created your preliminary watchlist, based on a mixture of technical and fundamental criteria, you can check out likely candidates for purchase, using detailed research. We'll cover this in the next chapter.

12

RESEARCH

With the exponential growth of available information on the internet, you will find that research, for us DIY-Investors, is a relatively straightforward task. Information easily available on the internet includes company websites, statutory accounts, news, broker's views and forecasts, bulletin boards, etc.

I've grouped research into the following topic areas:

12.1 Company's Story

Basic information that you should be looking for includes:

- What does the company do?
- How long has it been around?
- Where is it (FTSE 100, FTSE 350, small cap, fledgling, AIM)?
- Whereabouts is its business (UK, Europe, China, Worldwide)?
- Do the directors hold lots of shares?
- Are institutions and/or insiders (directors) holding lots of shares? (If so, what's the "free-float" of shares left for the rest of us?)
- Do any brokers cover the company (none or a low number is good)?
- If it has broker coverage, what are their recommendations and forecasts?
- Is there any recent news?

Overall, you need to get a feel of whether or not it's on the city radar screen. If it's not, that's good news for us DIY-Investors looking for low-priced, out of favour shares.

12.2 Fundamentals

We've looked, in chapter 9, at fundamental analysis but here I've listed (in no particular order) what you should be interested in:

- Length of trading history (beware of IPO prospectus documents!)
- Turnover
- MCAP
- PSR
- Profit (%)
- EPS
- Cash generation (PCF)
- Debt levels (and structure – short/long term)
- Dividends (if applicable)
- PE level (historical and prospective)
- PBV and PTBV
- Gearing
- Cash flow per share (compare it to EPS!)
- Depreciation
- Free cash per share
- Directors' holdings and recent transactions

12.3 News (RNS), Etc.

It's always good to "sniff around" for news and you'll need to check the following sources:

- RNS (covers issues that stock exchange rules require the company to publish)
- Company website, including any downloadable newsletters
- Notes contained in reports to the accounts (chairman's statement, director's report, etc.)
- Newspaper stories
- "Google search" – this sometimes brings up useful snippets of information

Finally, and often overlooked by the DIY-Investor, you can approach the company directly. Large companies will employ someone to deal with "investor relations" but for many small companies it is possible for you to speak to a director.

If you're lucky enough to get through to a director, don't waste their time. Do your homework first, including reading the latest accounts, and then prepare a list of questions.

12.4 Bulletin Boards

Most financial websites have bulletin boards, where any registered member (usually for free) can post messages. They can be a source of useful ideas and insights but they are also a place where you will find a lot of frivolous nonsense.

Occasionally, website links provided by contributors will take you to a piece of information that you haven't come across before.

However, occasionally you'll come across "rampers," people trying to artificially pump up the share price by expressing unsupported views as facts and in the worst case telling outright lies. My advice is to treat all information on bulletin boards with a degree of suspicion and views expressed are best taken with a large pinch of salt!

Finally, a quiet bulletin board or even better, one with recent negative comment can be a strong pointer to a company that is unloved and unwanted. This is positive news for us DIY-Investors, particularly when it is backed up by low valuations (by whatever measures you use).

12.5 Company Websites

Company websites can provide you with useful resources, including:

- Details of largest shareholders (holdings over 3%)
- Details of directors' shareholdings
- Information not on RNS statements (newsletters, biographies of directors, company history, etc.)
- Expanded detail on the company's activities and future intentions (significant items will be covered by RNS announcements)

12.6 Finally... Add to Watchlist?

As a result of the filtering process (covered in chapter 11) and your research, you should be in a position to either eliminate the company from your filtered list, or, alternatively, it may confirm the sort criteria. If so, you will want to add it to your watchlist portfolio on Sharescope. One thing that I do, is to add the date and current share price when I add a share to a watchlist portfolio. To do this, place your cursor on the grey (column heading) bar at the top of the watchlist portfolio. Then right click, select "Add general column" and select "Note." You can then add the information that you want to record and position this field where you wish. You can also rename the field (note) heading, to something more meaningful eg. 'Price when added'.

You may feel that this research process seems long winded but with practice, it becomes quick and easy to do. More importantly, it can be very rewarding financially!

Having created your watchlist, you're now ready to play the waiting game, monitoring the selection and getting ready to buy.

13

READY TO BUY? (MONITORING THE WATCHLIST – READY, STEADY, GO!)

What do you do after you have added a share to your watchlist? Well, what happens next can make all the difference between you making an average return, or a market-beating return on your investments. You need techniques and methods that can build your confidence as a DIY-Investor. Here are my suggestions ...

13.1 How to Monitor

By creating your watchlist on Sharescope, it is very easy to monitor regularly (daily or two or three times a week — you decide)!

You will find that it is very easy to set alerts to bring shares to your attention, when they meet your alert criteria. It could be a breakout (up or down) and within Sharescope, you can easily set an alarm. This could be set on a support or resistance line (which can be horizontal or sloping) and which can be a big help if you're pushed for time or monitoring a larger number of shares (say fifty to eighty).

My standard Sharescope view covers the last eighteen months. This works for me as primarily I'm interested in the recent history of the share price action. However, I have another view set to look at a much longer view — ten years' data (if available). I always like to view a multi-year chart, to make sure I get to see the big picture. You will be surprised at how often historical high or low prices repeat, as support or resistance levels.

You'll also look at the secondary indicators (volume, OBV, RSI, MACD, etc.) to get a feel as to what's happening. This will help you to get to know the stock.

13.2 Feeling the Pulse

This process of getting to know a company is what I call "feeling the pulse." It becomes more than a logical quantitative assessment as you begin to know and understand each candidate on your watchlist.

Common patterns begin to emerge, particularly with bruised, battered, or depressed shares. There are certain technical patterns that repeat and which you get to recognize. Even greater success comes from blending fundamental analysis and these common technical patterns, particularly when linked to the news stories (RNS, company websites, press comments, etc.).

13.3 Buy!

So what is it that triggers us to buy a particular share, rather than leave it sitting on the watchlist?

Not surprisingly, there is not a single (or simple) answer to this question. It depends on whether the stock is bruised, battered, or depressed. More importantly, it depends on your personal criteria and your "gut feel" about the company (the accuracy of this feeling improves with time)!

Over many years, I've noticed that the technical indicators can lead the fundamental indicators (or news) where the company is a fallen (bruised) blue chip or battered large company. However, with badly out-of-favour or depressed stocks, it can be the other way around — it seems to take ages for the share price to start moving up. Patience is a true virtue here!

Buy points can therefore come in many and varied different forms, such as:

- Breakout (subtle, significant, or explosive)
- Drift back or step down

- Retracement
- Good news (fundamental) – increase your holding?

It is through the use of technical analysis that you can get an edge...

13.4 TA Comes Into Its Own to Time Purchases

What you're looking for, as a DIY-Investor, is to be able to identify turning points. With the purchase of our winning shares we normally get two or three opportunities, so don't panic if you miss the first one.

There are also important clues and patterns that a turning point is happening, as noted in chapter 8, which will help you decide to buy.

By using Sharescope to monitor your watchlist, you will be able to spot breakouts. You may decide to use golden cross, breakout of trading range, breakthrough of a resistance level, or any other criteria you choose — to act as confirmation of buy signals.

Volume can also be a very significant factor in forming your judgment of the significance of the signal. A strong breakout supported by significantly-enhanced volume can be a strong positive indicator. However, remember that there is normally low volume on the more subtle breakouts (e.g. a lateral breakout from a long downtrend).

13.5 Current Trend?

One of the key reasons to have your potential buy candidates on a watchlist is to get an understanding of their price movements against the following:

- Short-term trend
- Medium- and long-term trends
- Moving averages
- Support and resistance levels
- Previous highs and lows

If you missed the initial buy point, you will also be very interested to observe if the share price has drifted back or stepped down to a support level. If so, this is your golden opportunity to buy (or to increase your holding, if you made an initial small investment).

13.6 What Do the Secondary Indicators Tell You?

The strength of your conviction to buy will be enhanced if several of the indicators are all reinforcing this view. The most common ones that I use are:

- Volume – if strong volume accompanies a breakout it is very positive
- RSI – rising RSI from an oversold position is a confirming signal
- OBV – a strong or preferably rising OBV is also a positive sign
- MACD – a buy signal (upward cross over) from an oversold position is positive
- Stochastics – a more complicated momentum indicator, this again uses the crossovers (up and down) as confirming signals. The relative position of the indicator (compared to the oversold line at 30 or overbought line at 70), as a measure of strength or weakness.

Positive divergence can also be a clue that the tide of sentiment on a share is turning. This occurs where a lower low on the daily share price graph is not matched by the action of the secondary indicators. For example, the RSI shows a higher low — hence positively diverging from the price action.

You will see from the following example (GTL Resources that we first came across as a depressed share in chapter 6), that there is positive divergence evident. This is marked by the black trend lines, downward in share price (from August 2008 to the end of April 2009) and the upward (positively diverging) trend line beneath the rising RSI indicator over the same period.

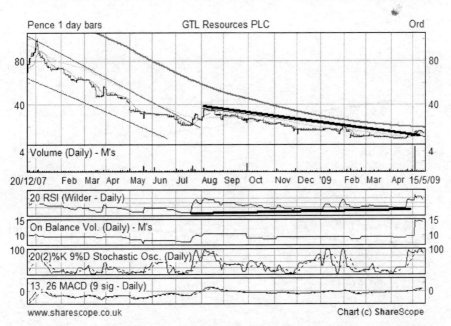

Fig. 13.1: GTL – Showing Positive Divergence (RSI and Price)

I've also noticed that there are occasionally trends that can be seen on indicators (such as OBV), which can be marked with a trend line on Sharescope. An upward breakout of that trend line on the secondary indicator can give a useful (sometimes leading) clue that some positive price movement may be about to happen. You can see this, again using GTL Resources as an example, in Fig. 13.2 (next page).

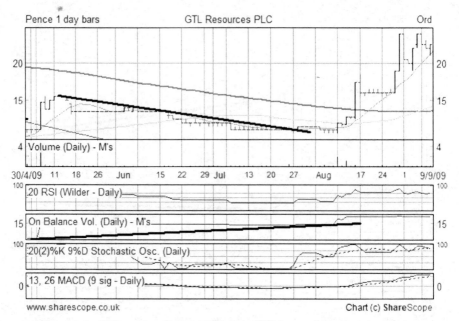

Fig. 13.2: GTL – Example of Rising OBV as a Leading Indicator

13.7 Good News!

The significance of an individual piece of good news will depend on whether the share is battered, bruised, or depressed. For the first two categories, there may be some positive buying action (and rise in share price) but for the depressed and disregarded stock, there is frequently no reaction at all. It is almost as if no one wants to believe the change in fortune, or perhaps it just means that the financial community has lost interest and isn't watching any more. Either way, it is another good opportunity for us DIY-Investors to pick up bargain low-priced shares that eventually become winners.

13.8 Pulling the Trigger

So that's it then, you've filtered and selected, monitored the watchlist, and now we're ready to buy — go pull the trigger (or press the return key) to make it happen. Or should we?

Here are some other factors to consider:

- **What is your target price to sell?**
  It is good practice to set yourself a price target, depending on your estimate of potential gain — relative to support and resistance levels. Alternatively, your target price level to sell may be when a particular fundamental level is reached (say PSR = 3.0).
- **How much are you going to invest?**
  Whether as a percentage of your investment pot, or in real (£) terms, how much will you invest? My minimum level for an investment is normally £1000 (to keep the charges reasonable in percentage terms). My maximum is 10% of my investment pot, for an initial purchase but I may increase to 20% with subsequent purchases (perhaps on the second buy point but only if I'm very positive on a stock).
- **What price will you buy at?**
  Some people like to set a target purchase price and will stick to it regardless (using a limit order). My approach is rather different. As I'm normally buying depressed or unloved stocks, I will normally buy at market prices. The reason is quite simple — with stocks that have bottomed out and are turning around, you may simply be waiting forever for the stock to drop to your purchase price. The caveat to this is that you've acted quickly when a buy signal (on your criteria) is met. What you want to avoid is buying at the end of a short-term (or even worse a medium-term) uptrend, only to watch in frustration as the price drifts down over the new few weeks or months.

13.9 What Next?

So there we are, you've bought your shares — what's next? Read on ...

14

MONITORING YOUR INVESTMENT PORTFOLIO

As a DIY-Investor, you need to keep a close watch on your money — remember, no one else is going to do it! So how do you go about monitoring your portfolio?

14.1 Portfolio Management

The first thing to say about portfolio management is that not all of your purchases will be winners (or at least not straight away). Read any investment book and they'll all say the same: some great stocks, some average, and one or two that perform very badly.

The aim is to, in overall terms, increase your wealth by picking winners. Key to this is being patient with your purchases. Give them time to appreciate in value and avoid damaging losses by weeding out your losers.

It's this last category where some people go so badly wrong. If a share drops, well below the purchase price (becoming a loser), some investors can't deal with being wrong. If you wait, believing you're right and the share price action is wrong, you may have even greater disappointment as the stock price drops even lower. Understanding that we can't be right all of the time is an important part of investing.

The key lesson is to learn from your mistakes, go back and re-evaluate what led you to make the buy decision, and (if necessary) refine your criteria. Watching a loser can be tremendously unnerving for the emotions and it is one of the best reasons for using a stop-loss on each share, particularly if you are new to investing.

14.2 Stop Losses

A stop loss acts like a safety net. Best of all, it can usually be set automatically (using your on-line broker's software) to automatically provide a passive way to protect your investments whilst you are going about your daily routine.

The key part about setting an automatic stop loss is to give the stock room to "wiggle." I would normally set a stop loss about 20–25% below my purchase price. So for example, if I've purchased £3,000 of XYZ company at 50p per share (to own about 6,000 shares), I will normally set the stop loss at about 40p (20% below the purchase price).

If however there is a support line say at 38p, I would normally set the stop loss below this level (say at 35p) i.e. 30% below my purchase price. The reason for this is that sometimes the share price (intra-day) may drop down to a previous support line before bouncing back up to close the day at a higher level. Some people believe that market makers (stockbrokers) manipulate the bid price, which will trigger your stop loss, to suit their own needs. Perhaps this is too cynical a view but there are sometimes some very erratic price movements during a trading day.

One other time when stop losses come into their own, is if you go on holiday. This is particularly so if you are abroad or don't have internet access during your vacation. Stop losses, at least on your largest holdings, do offer some level of comfort that your investments are protected while you are away.

14.3 Tweaking the Mix

I touched earlier on how much to invest in one particular holding. The whole subject of your portfolio concentration, or diversification, is very important.

One of the key areas of your overall wealth management is how to divide your assets. Will you invest in property, bonds, shares, commodities, physical things (art, coins, rare stamps, etc.) and in what proportions?

Within the context of this book we'll assume that your investment portfolio refers to the proportion of your assets invested in shares (stocks).

Over a period of time, it is good to refine your system. The best advice that I can offer is to read widely and form your own view (see recommended reading list in appendix 2). I believe that as DIY-Investors, it is up to us to have a system that suits our personality. We then need to stick to it, perhaps refining it gradually based on our own experience.

My own investment rules allow me to:

- Invest up to 10% of my portfolio in one share (initially). Then if I add to this holding, which normally means the share price has gone up, invest further funds to total a maximum of 20% of my portfolio. *(Note: If this percentage increases, as a result of a strong rise in the shareprice, this is acceptable — run the winners, cut the losers!)*
- Dip my toe in the water for the more speculative (read "riskier") stocks, with a minimum investment of £1,000.
- Add to my holdings at higher prices, if fundamental analysis and/ or company news confirms a turnaround in fortunes (removing, or reducing the risk which may have been present when I initially invested).
- Take profits by selling part of a holding, if I believe there is another prospect that warrants investment.
- Sell all of one holding if the valuation gets too high (by my criteria — see chapter 15 on selling).
- Be flexible in my approach according to intermediate and major trends in the stock market as a whole.

One other aspect for you to consider when reviewing your portfolio is the question "Would I buy this stock now?" If the answer is no, should you still have it?

14.4 How to Monitor Your Portfolio

This process is much the same as monitoring your watchlist (see chapter 13), the big difference is it's real money at stake, and it's yours!

In addition to the techniques listed in chapter 13, the main things you're looking for are:

- Any negative news (but use your own judgment on the significance of this).
- Are there any signs of over-valuation on a fundamental basis (particularly a high PSR)?
- If so, are there any technical signs of a change in trend (from up to down, or up to sideways)? Again the significance will depend on your target timescale for holding this stock.
- A "gut feeling"* that something has changed.

*This "gut feeling" is where investing crosses from the scientific, tangible, logical world to intuition and the sub-conscious mind. I can only describe this state as feeling either good or bad about an investment. Note that it only comes about by observing and knowing your portfolio of investments and candidates on your watchlist. It also improves with time!

14.5 Getting News on Your Companies

In addition to the use of your broker's account (to get RNS announcements) and the Sharescope news feature, tune in to your companies by:

- Subscribing to news directly from your companies (via their websites)
- Tuning in to the financial press (Investors Chronicle and Financial Times, etc. (or their on-line content, by subscription)
- Read bulletin boards (but make your own mind up on the content!)
- Don't forget the occasional search (using Google, Yahoo, or similar) in case there is useful content on-line not easily available elsewhere

14.6 Happy to Hold?

The main objective of the periodic review of your portfolio holdings is for you to answer the question, for each stock, "Am I happy to hold?"

My approach is to hold, unless:

- The story changes (for the worse)
- Company financials deteriorate
- The stock is overvalued (by PSR)
- Technical indicators give a shove (e.g. breaking down through a trend line)!
- There are better opportunities elsewhere (but only when I've made money — not because I'm impatient)

If the answer to the question "Happy to hold?" is no, then we need to consider the important, but often overlooked, topic of selling …

15

SELLING

This is the least written-about part of investing and yet it is where your profits are made real. Up to this point, the gain from an appreciating share price is merely a "paper profit." Conversely of course any paper loss is only made real, crystallised as some would say, by a sale.

15.1 Selling Manually or Automatically?
Selling can be more emotional than buying. When buying a share, you have done your research and have expectations of future rises in the share price. There is hope, anticipation, and perhaps confidence in your choice.

Selling should normally be due to one of three reasons:

- Your price target (gain) has been met
- You want to sell part of a holding, at a gain, re-investing the proceeds in another stock that you wish to own (or increase your holding in)
- Your stop loss price has been met (or triggered if set automatically)

When selling to "cut your losses" (which in reality means preventing greater losses), this can be done automatically or manually. Done manually, you need to be aware of likely feelings of despair ("I got it wrong!") and an emotional feeling of loss. It may sound harsh but you have to get used to it. Investing involves taking losses as well as making gains. None of us gets it right all of the time.

Much has been written on the psychology of winning and losing, in relation to investing as well as other walks of life. A detailed exploration would be out of place here, in this "how to" book, but I have included a list of some well-regarded texts on the subject in appendix 2 (recommended reading).

One of the best ways of taking emotion out of the selling process is to use good-till-cancelled (GTC) sell orders on your on-line broking platform, assuming you are using an execution-only broker. Traditional brokers will normally operate GTC sell orders as well, for those investors using a full-service brokerage.

One of the main advantages of a GTC order for the DIY-Investor is that you can go about your daily business without having to worry. You can even go away on holiday, having set up your GTC orders. This is particularly useful if you want to set protective stop losses to safeguard against sudden falls whilst you're away.

15.2 Holding Winners and Cutting Losers

For all investors, the aim is to pick winners but why do we always want to get out too early? The old saying about not going bust by taking a profit is all well in theory. However, if you sell too early, you can miss out on the really big gains (2x to 10x or more).

We can learn a lot from great investors like Warren Buffett, Peter Lynch, Ken Fisher, etc. By running their winners, they each consistently created market-beating returns. All will have had their share of mistakes but it is by finding great investments, and sticking with them, that they consistently come out as winners.

As DIY-Investors then, what techniques and tools can we use to decide when to sell and at what price?

15.3 Deciding to Sell

Remembering that our aim is to pick winning shares by investing in bruised, battered, or depressed companies, how do we know when to sell?

One obvious pointer is that the previously unloved stock is now in favour with the city and/or the financial press. However, before jumping off because everyone else seems to be getting on board remember the following points:

- When the investment tide turns positive (after a long period of negative sentiment) the upward reaction can continue for some time
- Genuine turn-around situations can produce some of the largest gains of all winners on the stock market (given enough time). Don't get off too early!

One of the most reliable fundamental measures of over-valuation of a share is a high PSR (price-to-sales ratio). This does depend on the type of business that the company is in and also its size (MCAP).

By analysing the high and low PSR's of an individual company for previous years, you can get a feeling of previous highs and lows. Thus if you have bought at a low PSR and, after riding the gain, the PSR gets to a high level (relative to past high levels) then consider selling. I have included as a case study in chapter 16 West China Cement, where after making considerable gains, I used PSR analysis to make the sell decision (backed up by technical analysis).

If you are already using a trailing stop loss, you might consider "tightening the stop" i.e. reducing the amount that the price has to fall before triggering the GTC sell order.

However, where the turnover grows rapidly, PSR analysis will also reveal that the company is not overvalued, i.e. its PSR ratio is within the normal range for the share (based on historic analysis).Further clues can be gained from one or more technical indicators such as:

- A break down through a trend line
- Price falling through a support level
- Secondary indicators showing "overbought" or "negative divergence"
- A price reversal signal

15.4 Stop Losses

Unless you monitor your investments daily, stop losses should be a tool that you use in your investing. Stop losses are normally "good till cancelled" (GTC) and will sit in place, acting as a safety net to protect against sudden falls in share price.

I have used stop losses and still do occasionally, even though I monitor my investments daily. One key part of the "setting" of the sell price is to leave what I call "wiggle room" for the normal share price fluctuation. Even then, occasionally a large fall during the day (intra-day) may trigger the stop loss order. Even more frustratingly, when this happens, the share price will climb during the latter part of the day — closing above your stop loss level. Again, just accept that this will occasionally happen. Before moving on though, go back and examine where you set your stop loss (trigger) price to see if any lessons can be learned.

Stop losses can be used for one (or more) of the following reasons:

- If you are new to investing or have a nervous disposition (note: this nervousness will pass in time as you get used to the normal gyrations of the stock market).
- You are going on holiday and want to leave a safety net in place to guard against sudden losses (from whatever reason).
- If you want to lock in a profit at a certain level. For example if a share has increased by (say) 70% and you think it is looking overbought. You could set a stop loss at a level that would lock in a gain of 50%.
- You want to take the emotion out of the selling process. This is one of the best reasons for using stop losses (whether at a fixed price or a trailing stop loss).

Trailing Stop Losses

This type of stop loss is set at a given amount (pence) or percentage below the current share price. As the share price increases the stop level (trigger price for the sale) moves up with it. Once increased, it stays at this higher level until either it is triggered and the GTC sale order kicks in, or it is dragged up by the share price rising still further.

As mentioned before, take care with this type of order to leave the "wiggle room" that I mentioned.

15.5 Pre-Set Sell Orders

A pre-set sell order is again another type of good-till-cancelled (GTC) order. Normally the intention is to lock in a given percentage gain (usually set as a target).

For example, if you buy 500 shares of XYZ Company for £2.20 each and after a few months the share price is up to £3.08 (a gain of 40%). You might feel that, at a gain of 50%, you wish to sell. This could be because you have identified a better prospect from amongst your watchlist. You therefore set a GTC sell order for the 500 shares at £3.30 (for the 50% gain).

A second example might be a battered and depressed share, that you have identified as an excellent prospect as a long-term hold. You have bought (perhaps last year) 4,000 shares at 50p and now they trade at £1.05 per share. You believe that they may be temporarily overbought (as a result of studying the share price graph and technical indicators). You therefore set a GTC order for 2,000 shares, half of your holding, at a price of £1.10 per share. If this is triggered, you have taken your original investment stake "off the table" — leaving the profit on the trade at risk (hopefully short term).

Of course, one important aspect here to consider is the capital gain that you realise (assuming the investment vehicle is subject to capital gains tax). Good record keeping is essential here to provide information for your tax returns, even if prepared by a third party on your behalf. This is covered in more detail in chapter 17.

15.6 Dealing with the Proceeds of Sales

The first, and perhaps most important rule here, is not to be in a panic to buy the next stock just because you have some money from a sale.

Go back to your watchlist and evaluate the possibilities. For any possible candidate, go through the following quick checklist:

- Check the share price graph (including secondary technical indicators)
- Check recent news, particularly if any results have been released. Has the story changed in any way?
- Check director selling — large sales by a director, or more significantly, by more than one director, would be good reason to delay the purchase

Remember to look at the trend of the overall market. If it has been in an uptrend but has just broken down, through a trend line, it may be best to wait.

Don't forget that there may be further buying opportunities on another share that you already hold — it may be the winning pick of your investments!

By this point in the book, you have had to absorb a lot of information. In the next chapter, I'll illustrate some of the points made so far, in a practical way and in the context of real companies that became "winning shares" for me.

16

CASE STUDIES

Having read the preceding chapters, you are probably wondering how to put all of this into practice. Here, I'll show you how — by way of case studies. You will read about my thought processes and see my approach to being a DIY-Investor. I'll try and convey what my feelings were, at the time, about the prospects for each company that is covered. You will see that these examples cover the four main categories that I discussed in chapter 6, namely:

- Bruised "big un's" (Xstrata)
- The tide's out (Vedanta Resources)
- Depressed stocks (Real Good Food Group)
- Post-IPO fallers (Entertainment One)

16.1 Xstrata (Epic: XTA)
Xstrata (XTA) is a miner, producing coal, zinc, and other metal alloys. It is also a member of the FTSE 100.

This company appeared on my "radar" as a possible candidate, as a result of using my Sharescope screen, for shares down by more than 75% in the past twelve months.

From its high of £25.017 (19th May 2008), it had dropped by 88% to its low of £2.983 (9th March 2009). This compared to a fall of 44.4% by the FTSE 100, from 6376.5 to 3542.4, over the same period.

Xstrata was (and is) a company that grew through acquisition, as well as organic growth. On the 6th August 2008, it had announced a possible bid for fellow FTSE 100 member Lonmin — at a price of £33 per share (Lonmin's price had been £23.19 per share immediately prior to the announcement). As the tide of investment sentiment had turned and went out during autumn 2008, Xstrata was forced to announce (1st October 2008) that it had no intention to bid for Lonmin "… due to the current unprecedented uncertainty in the financial markets …" As a result, Xstrata was badly "bruised" as investors turned against it. As is often the case with a heavyweight company (its MCAP in May 2008 was £24 billion), it had "overshot" on the downside.

Fig.16.1: Xstrata – Break of Trend and Subsequent Decline

The clear break, below the 200-day SMA in July 2008, had been a clear warning to the observant investor. As the leaves of the autumn fell in 2008, so did most of the constituent members of the FTSE 100 but Xstrata was particularly badly hit. It had been badly "bruised"!

Looking at the decline (see Fig. 16.2), you will note that the fall was in three stages. XTA suffered a steady decline for the first two months, then the rate of fall was much steeper for the next two months. Finally, it entered a more gradual "tail off" over the next five months (November 2008 to March 2009). This "bottoming process" is worthy of closer examination.

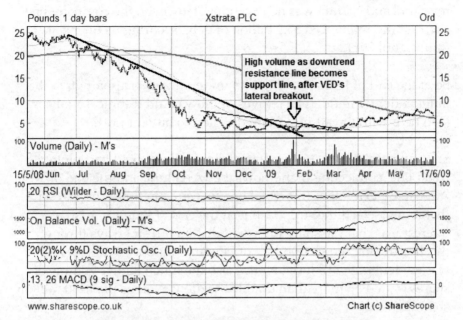

Fig.16.2: Xstrata – The "Bottoming Process"

From the graph (Fig. 16.2), you can clearly see that there is support at the £3 per share price level. This is not surprising. Based on a range of measures, Xstrata was undervalued.

The Xstrata annual results, for the year ending 31st December 2008 (preliminary results released 29th January 2009), showed turnover of £19.168 billion (equivalent to £11.34 per share).

Thus, at the low point £2.983 (9th March 2009), it traded on the following valuations:

PSR	=	0.26	(£2.983/£11.34)
PCF	=	1.12	(£2.983/£2.672)
PE	=	1.73	(£2.983/£1.727)

What had unnerved investors was the high level of debt, in the context of the world banking crisis. This had caused the company to cancel its final dividend. This is always going to be badly received by

127

investors and Xstrata was no exception. However, the company had successfully refinanced $5.5 billion of debt, securing its financial future until 2011.

So at the end of January 2009, with undervaluation apparent, to the independently minded DIY-Investor, how could technical analysis (TA) help with the all-important decision to buy (or not)?

From the graph (Fig. 16.3 opposite), you can see that I had plotted a trend line, connecting higher lows, between June and the end of August. By extending this trend line forwards in time, you can see that it intersected the support line at the end of January. Also of interest was that the share price had drifted out sideways through this line during the second half of January and once again support was evident at the £3 level. Notice also the much higher volume of shares traded — more than double the daily average of 30–40 million shares.

The spike in volume seemed to confirm the bottom. However, you will also see that another (short-term) trend line was in place. This connected higher lows between the beginning of November and the beginning of January. If the SP cleared this line, it would be reasonable to assume a new uptrend was in place.

However, this line proved to be stubborn resistance for a few more weeks. It seemed to act like a sloping ceiling that the price couldn't break through.

That changed with the rights issue (March 2009) which raised £4.1 billion to reduce the level of debt that XTA was carrying. On higher volume, in the second week of March 2009, XTA broke through the resistance line. You will also see from the secondary indicators below the graph (Fig 16.2) that there was a buy signal on the Stochastic Oscillator and that the on-balance volume (OBV) started to show increased strength (by turning up).

You will also notice that, as the new uptrend broke through the 200-day moving average, there was a minor reversal for about five weeks to the second week of July 2009. At this point, XTA kicked off again, resuming its uptrend. This move would last through to spring 2010 and would see the share price top £12 — a fourfold increase in the share price in the 12-month period (see Fig. 16.3 below).

Fig.16.3: Xstrata – Breakout and Recovery

Xstrata would have also fitted the category of shares, covered in chapter 6, entitled "The Tide's Out," which we'll look at next.

16.2 Vedanta Resources (Epic: VED)

Vedanta Resources (VED) is also a member of the FTSE 100 and therefore qualifies as a "blue chip" company, albeit a relatively new member of this elite group. It is classified as a mining company but its activities include producing iron, copper, zinc, lead, and aluminum. Based mainly in India, it is well-placed geographically to service markets in India, China, and surrounding countries.

Although I had owned Vedanta during various periods, between 2004 and mid 2006 (as a growth share), it had disappeared off my radar screen during 2007 and 2008. The reasons for this were quite simple: I had made good returns (more than doubling my money) and I felt that there were better returns to be made elsewhere. Now you might argue that I had missed out a substantial gain as the share price had again doubled, from £12 to £27+ (May 2008). However, by my criteria and particularly on a PSR basis, it had become overvalued (it had a PSR of 2.2 on the 30th May 2008).

Also relevant was the direct impact that the growing storm clouds of the banking crisis were having on the FTSE 100. From a high point of 6730.7 (12th October 2007), the FTSE 100 was drifting lower and seemed to me be unable to clear and stay above the 200-day moving average. A pattern of "lower highs" was now evident on the FTSE 100 graph (see Fig. 16.4 below).

Fig.16.4: FTSE 100 – Decline from 2008 to Spring 2009

Now, normally I'm not a big watcher of what the FTSE 100 index is doing, but, if you're considering one of its members as a possible investment, then clearly you need to be aware of what's happening.

As the summer unfolded and we moved into autumn, Vedanta suffered. It's share price fell from a high of £27.80 (19th May 2008) and would eventually bottom out at 387.75p (20th Nov 2008). This represented a fall of 86% in six months — very definitely "out with the tide."

130

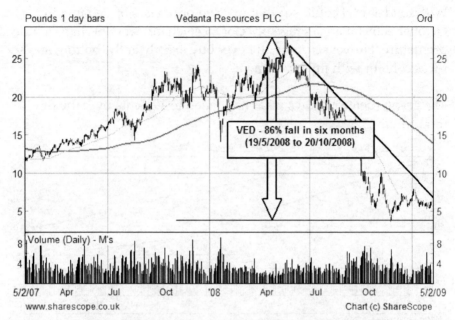

Fig.16.5: Vedanta – Decline from May to October 2008

By comparison, it is interesting to note that the FTSE 100 fell from 6376.5 to 3875.0 over the same period — a fall of 39.2%. Again, the tendency for over-reaction, this time to the downside, was evident.

Thus, at the low point £3.8775 (20th November 2008), it traded on the following valuations (earnings and cashflow based on the annual accounts to 31st March 2008):

PSR	=	0.27	(£3.8775/£14.36)
PCF	=	0.95	(£3.8775/£4.09)
PE	=	2.81	(£3.8775/£1.38)

Vedanta's turnover, for the 12 months to 31st March 2008, was £4.134 billion. This gave a turnover per-share value of £14.36. At the bottom (November 2008), Vedanta's PSR was 0.27. With a PCF of 0.95 and a PE of 2.81, it was very firmly on the radar screen, for DIY-Investors using PSR, PCF or PE analysis as a valuation measure.

With hindsight, I could see that my two purchases of Vedanta in October 2008 (at an average price of £6.46/share) were perhaps a little premature. However, you will never buy exactly at the bottom and so I was content with my investment.

The graph (below) shows what happened to Vedanta over the few months.

Fig.16.6: Vedanta – Bottoming Process and Lateral Breakout

For the next four months, from its base in November 2008, VED moved sideways (see Fig. 16.6, above). Note these three important points:

- A sideways pattern (triangle) developed with a horizontal base at about £5
- In early February 2009, Vedanta moved out (and up) through the extended resistance line, marking the "lower highs" from May to September 2008
- In the middle of March 2009, VED crept sideways through the resistance line marking the "lower highs" of the triangle that had formed over the past five months

From where I sat, this was very bullish for Vedanta. Over the next four months, Vedanta's share price began to rebound.

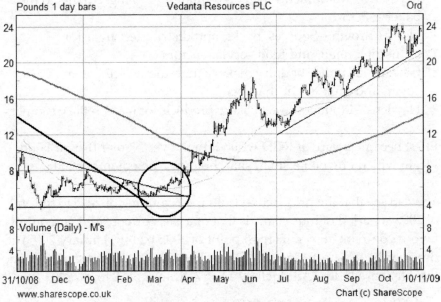

Fig.16.7: Vedanta – Breakout and Recovery

As the rebound continued, I sold my share in four trenches at an average price of £12.50 per share.

The result of this investment? A gain of 93% in nine months. Could I have made a larger gain? Well, yes is the answer (with the benefit of hindsight) but I had then met my objective of a 50% gain on the rebound of Vedanta. My own preference is for larger gains from depressed and out-of-favour stocks. However, the short-term opportunity on Vedanta was too tempting to miss.

16.3 The Real Good Food Group (Epic: RGD)
The Real Good Food Group (RGD) is an AIM-listed food manufacturing and distribution business. Following incorporation in February 2003, it made its first acquisitions in July 2003. Flotation on the Alternative Investment Market (AIM) followed in September 2003.

RGD has four main strands to its business:

- Renshaw – Manufacturer of high-quality food ingredients to the bakery sector
- Napier Brown – Sources, packs, and distributes sugar for industrial, retail, and food service sectors
- Garrett – Supplier of dairy, bakery ingredients, ice-cream mixes, sugar, and milk to UK markets
- Haydens – Produces sweet bakery products for major retail customers

I first became aware of RGD when it took over Napier Brown Food Plc, in which I owned a small shareholding, in September 2005.

You can see that the price action from the beginning of 2005 to the end of 2008, a period of four years, is that of a classic depressed and out-of-favour company. From its high point of 193.5p (14th January 2005), it dropped by 99% to 1.625p (3rd December 2008). Over the same period, the All-Share Index (ASX) fell by 14.35% (from 2420.2 to 2078.8).

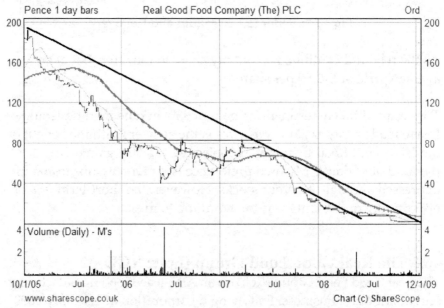

Fig. 16.8: Real Good Food – Four-Year Decline

You can see from the graph (Fig 16.8, above) that the "bottoming process" showed a gradual flattening out during 2008. The banking crisis during the autumn of 2008 contributed to a dramatic slump in the share price which then "bumped along" for two months at around 2.5 to 2.0 pence, before hitting its low of 1.625 pence on 3rd December. RGD then started to show signs of life (see Fig. 16.9, below).

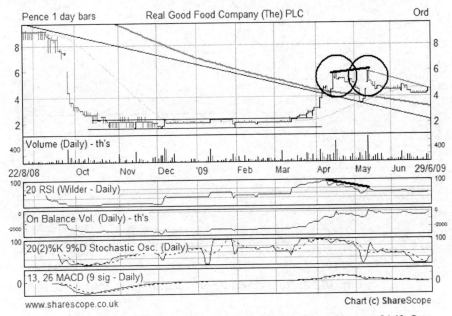

Fig. 16.9: Real Good Food – Spring 2009 – First Signs of Life?

There are several points of interest for you to observe, from the above graph, as follows:

- The 50-day moving average provides considerable resistance until the SP breaks decisively through this during the last two weeks of March 2009.
- The short-term rise, breaking the 200-day SMA (on higher volume), quickly reverses in April, with the price just below the 6p level (note low-high, high-low reversal bars on 17th and 18th April 2009).
- As the price moves back down, it bounces off a strong resistance line. This is the forward extension of the line, marking lower highs, during 2008.
- This bounce is interesting. Despite the gap up, there is negative divergence on both RSI & MACD (secondary TA indicators) —

shown on Fig. 16.9. There is also another low-high, high-low pair of OHLC bars on 13th/14th May 2009, representing another reversal signal.

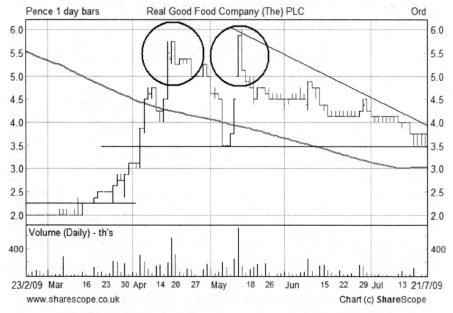

Fig. 16.10: Real Good Food – April/May 2009

- At this point, the DIY-Investor should have been on their guard and may even take some profits. This will of course depend on whether you are in for the long term, or trading actively over a shorter timescale.

The price action then followed a typical "drift back," which you will recall from chapter 8, through to July 2009. On 24th July, with sharply increased volume, the next breakout occurred. You may have noticed at this point that the 200-day SMA also starts to turn up.

This short-term move took the share price to 8.125p (6th August 2009) but at this point the price is well above the 200-day SMA which is now gently sloping up. In a fashion typical of the recovery of a depressed stock, there is another low-high, high-low reversal and the SP starts to drift back down (see Fig 16.11, opposite).

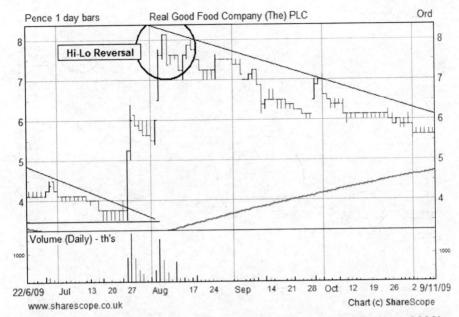

Fig. 16.11: Real Good Food – Breakout and Reversal (July/Aug 2009)

As the price gently falls over the next few weeks, it becomes obvious that there is a clear sloping resistance line joining the lower highs. This lasts through to 26th January 2010 (see Fig 16.12, below). Note how the breakout at this point is again marked by high volume (3.1m shares). Over the next few weeks, there is a more positive pair of bullish zig-zag moves, resembling stair-steps. This is followed by another "explosive breakout" on 11th March 2010, with very high volume of 4.2m shares traded.

This almost doubles the price in a matter of days and marks a strong upward move, which lasts through to 10th June 2010. You will note reversal bars (again) at this point, which together with the distance of the price above the 200-day SMA would suggest a period of consolidation, as we move into the autumn of 2010.

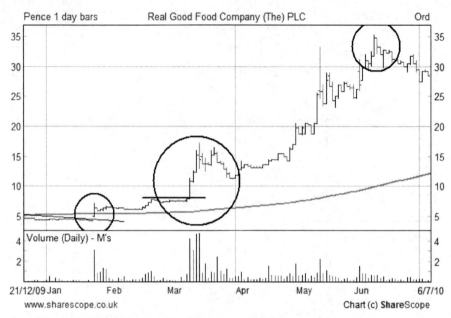

Fig. 16.12: Real Good Food – Spring/Summer 2010

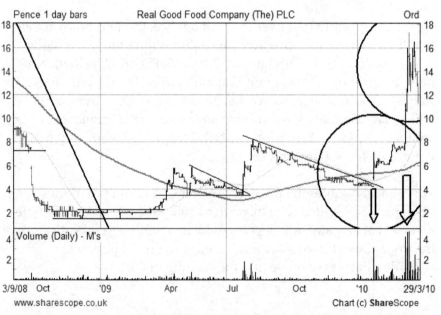

Fig. 16.13: Real Good Food – Repeated Patterns during 2009–2010

You can see that applying the techniques contained in this book, there were good returns to be made from RGD in both 2009 and 2010.

16.4 Entertainment One (Epic: ETO)

Entertainment One (LSE: ETO) was another company that first came to my attention when it appeared on my Sharescope filter screen, for shares down by more than 75% in the past 12 months. This was June 2009 and, at that time, ETO was listed on the Alternative Investment Market (AIM).

It had joined AIM in March 2007, following a placing and subscription of 80 million shares at £1 per share. ETO is a media company specialising in acquisition, production, and distribution of film and televisions content. It also licenses merchandising in connection with its television and film rights.

You may well have come across the books and films of the three-part "Twilight Saga" (*Twilight* and *New Moon* being the first two — both box-office successes). ETO also has a successful range of family and children's content, including *The Gruffalo* and *Peppa Pig*.

You will recall from chapter 6, the reasons that many post-IPO companies have a tough time, in terms of their share price action. Typically, the share price of ETO had fallen in the first few months of its publicly-traded existence on AIM (see Fig.16.11, below).

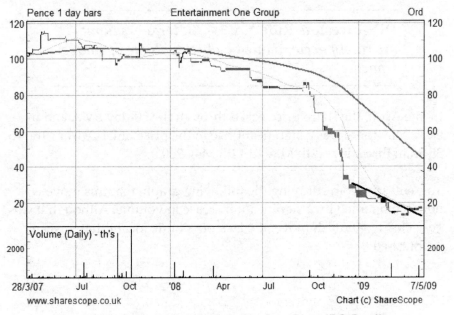

Fig. 16.11: Entertainment One Group – Post-IPO Decline

The rate of decline accelerated during the autumn of 2008, amidst the general uncertainty of the banking crisis. The decline then began to slow, as ETO entered 2009, and the price bottomed at 13.5p — holding at this level for five days (26th March to 1st April 2009).

From its post-IPO high of 115p (25th April 2007), ETO had fallen 88.2% to 13.5p. During the same period, the All-Share Index (ASX) had fallen from 3359.4 to 1906.8 on 30th March 2009. This represented a fall of 43.2%. Clearly ETO had significantly underperformed the index.

However, one note of confidence was the proposed partial cash offer by Marwyn Neptune Fund, who were prepared to offer 12.5p per share in cash to acquire a further 27 million shares from ordinary shareholders of ETO. To the alert DIY-Investor, this was time to sit up and take notice.

Another bullish factor was the lateral breakout of ETO's share price during March 2009. The line of resistance, connecting lower highs during 2008, was quietly left behind as the share price moved sideways during March and April 2009.

DIY-Investors Rule No. 3 – *"lateral breakouts" are rarely accompanied by high volume of shares traded.*

In late April, the share price eased through the 50-day SMA and in early May there was a significant rise in the price of ETO, from 16p to 35.5p in three days (7th May to 12th May 2009).

You will see, from studying the following graph, that this move was not accompanied by a significant increase in volume. Although it was very clearly a bullish move, the lack of volume meant that it wasn't "confirmed."

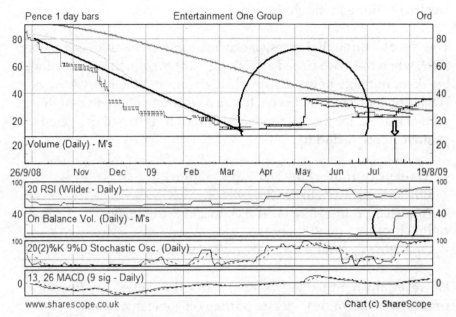

Fig. 16.12: Entertainment One Group – First Signs of Recovery

My reading of the situation in June 2009 was that the share price could well drift back further. Looking at the secondary indicators after the doubling of the share price in May (see Fig. 16.12), it was apparent to me that the RSI and stochastic indicators were both suggesting that ETO was overbought. In this situation, I normally place a horizontal line at the previous high (35.5p in this case). This is a hurdle that I'm looking for the share price to clear to confirm the uptrend is firmly in place.

Prior to ETO clearing this hurdle, a very positive signal was the high volume (27.43 million shares) traded on 22nd July 2009. This was followed over the next few days by the price moving through the short-term resistance line (May–June 2009). This was backed up by confirmation by all four secondary indicators (RSI, OBV, stochastic, and MACD).

From the graph (Fig. 16.12), you can see that the price moved steadily upwards, through the 200-day SMA, before halting on 13th August, with the price closing at 35.25p. The horizontal line drawn at 35.5p, from the high on 12th May, then provided resistance for the next four weeks, resulting in the share price going sideways.

The "break" through this resistance line came on the 10th September 2009, when the price closed at 37.0p (up 2p). Again, this was a quiet breakout but note how consistently high (strong) the RSI, OBV, and stochastic indicators had been. It's also worth mentioning that the annual results, for the year ended 31st March 2009, had delivered positive news, including:

- Revenue (turnover) up 29.6% to £342.6m
- EBITDA up 35.6% to £25.3m
- Adjusted profit before tax (PBT) up 27.1% to £16.4m
- EPS up 12.5% (to 8.1 pence)
- Operating cash flow up 25.1% (to £35.9m)

However, the reported loss before tax of £31.0 million (up from the prior loss of £7.7m) was clearly putting off some investors.

In reality, it was the "impairment charges" (a non-cash adjustment by the directors) of £25.2m as a "one-off" adjustment that had the dual effect of reducing stated pre-tax profits and, at the same time reducing some of the intangible book value.

Following these results and with (diluted) total shares outstanding of 138.4 million, the market capitalisation (MCAP) at the breakout point (10th September 2009) was £51.2 million.

Using the annual results (to 31st March 2009) gave the following fundamental valuation measures:

PSR	=	0.15	(£51.2m / £342.6m)
PCF	=	1.43	(£51.2m / £35.9m)
PE	=	-2.51	(37p / -14.72p)
PBV	=	0.38	(£51.2m / 133.2m)
PTBV	=	-0.95	(£51.2m / £ -53.9m)

At 31st March 2009, an independent third party report had valued ETO's film, television, and music library at $220 million (£153 million at the 31/3/2009 exchange rate). By investing in ETO, you were picking up £3 of value in this "library" for every £1 spent — clearly a bargain!

The share price action during the second half of 2009 and through 2010 (so far), shows that ETO is very clearly in an uptrend channel. A line joining higher highs marks the upper (resistance) line of the channel and the upward sloping 200-day simple moving average (SMA) is likely to mark the lower (support) line of the channel. ETO has also joined the main London Stock Exchange (LSE), which the company hopes will improve liquidity and benefit shareholders.

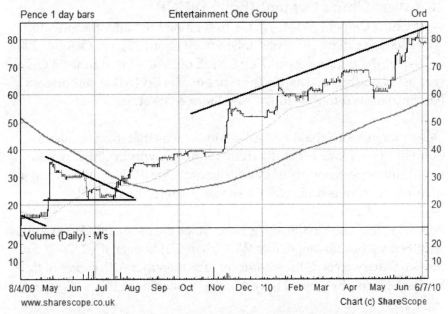

Fig. 16.13: Entertainment One Group – Uptrend Firmly in Place!

You might well be saying "How will I know when to sell ETO?" Well, as DIY-Investors, we must each make up our own mind but my approach, detailed in chapter 15, is that I will:

- Monitor the share price graph, selling if there is significant break below the 200-day moving average.
- Keep a watch on any RNS releases for ETO. Should any bad news arise, I'll watch the share price action even more carefully.

- Look at each set of interim and annual results, and calculate the rolling turnover. For example, after the interim results take the second half turnover (from the previous annual results less the previous year's first half turnover), then add this to the current interim results. Work out the PSR and compare both to historical PSR results for ETO and to the sector and market as a whole. If the PSR gets as high as 3.0, I may decide to sell my shares, or at least a proportion of them.
- ETO is likely to become a classic growth share but my intention is to retain my investment until I judge it to be overvalued.

16.5 West China Cement (Epic: WCC)

West China Cement (AIM: WCC), first gained my attention in late April 2008. Its share price had fallen from about 255p in October 2007, to 104p at the bottom (April 2008), a fall of 59%. At that time, WCC was listed on the Alternative Investment Market (AIM), although it has since moved to the Hong Kong Stock Market.

One of the reasons that I had taken notice was that, from a macro point of view, I knew that the tremendous growth in China was going to require huge amounts of infrastructure. One of the key components to infrastructure is concrete — hence my interest in cement.

Following the move to the Hong Kong Stock Exchange (HKEx) in August 2010, Sharescope no longer lists WCC shares. However, my DIY-Investors diary records the significant facts, together with copies of the Sharescope graphs which I have scanned to include in this section.

We begin the story in late May, when the share price had started to pick up, breaking up through the downtrend line (see Fig. 16.14, below).

My first purchase took place in June 2008, at a price of 148p per share. Over the next eighteen months, the share price appreciated significantly. This was partly helped by the Chinese government's financial stimulus package, initiated during autumn 2008 in response to the world banking crisis. The catastrophic earthquake, on 12th May 2008, in the Sichuan province had also increased the demand for cement, to rebuild the local infrastructure, housing, and economy.

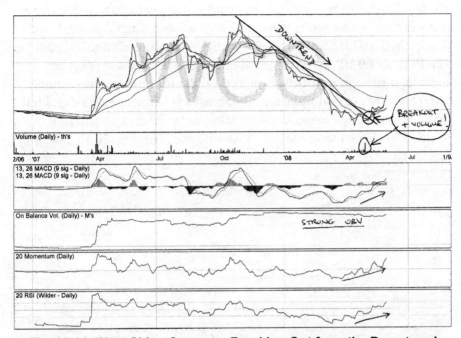

Fig. 16.14: West China Cement – Breaking Out from the Downtrend

For some weeks after my purchase, the share price remained broadly flat, until in late July it started to move up significantly. Eager to invest in another share, in late July, I somewhat prematurely sold part of my holding. The lesson here is to be aware of when the next set of results are due — something that seemed to have temporarily deserted me!

The interim results, released on 28th August 2009, really gave WCC a boost. Cement sales had increased by 26%, the turnover was up by 70%, and operating profit had increased by 121%. Consequently, the balance of my shares in WCC moved sharply on upwards and by the time I had sold the balance, the overall gain had been 110.76% in just under six months.

The share price did move even higher, spiking at the top in late October at £4.91. I moved WCC back to my watchlist, where I continued to monitor developments.

On 1st February 2010, I noticed that there was an apparent high-low, low-high reversal (just above the upward sloping 200-day moving

145

average line). The Sharescope financial summary (see opposite page) showed that the earnings were expected to more than double, from 38.45p (Y/E 31/12/2008) to 78.63p for the year just ended (31/12/2009). The PEG was 0.10, a strong signal of growth and I was expecting continued growth in turnover, based on the interim results (August 2009) and the general upbeat news about the Chinese economy. I felt that it was time to consider re-investing in WCC and, as usual, I decided to check the secondary TA indicators (see Fig. 16.15, below).

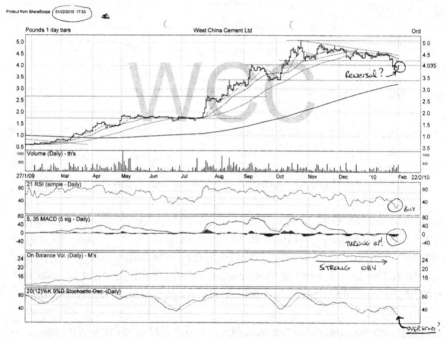

Fig. 16.15: West China Cement – February 2010, the Second Purchase

I discovered that the signals were a little mixed. RSI was indicating a "buy"and the MACD indicator looked as though it was starting to turn up, although it wasn't really down in oversold territory. However, the stochastic indicator was oversold and the OBV was strong and had just turned up on the high-low, low-high reversal. I decided to watch for a few more days but on 11th February, it was clear to me that a new upward move was starting. I purchased a new holding at a price of £4.69 per share. After just four weeks, I sold part of my holding and after a further six weeks (just ten weeks after the purchase), with the share price at £6.76, I judged that it was time to

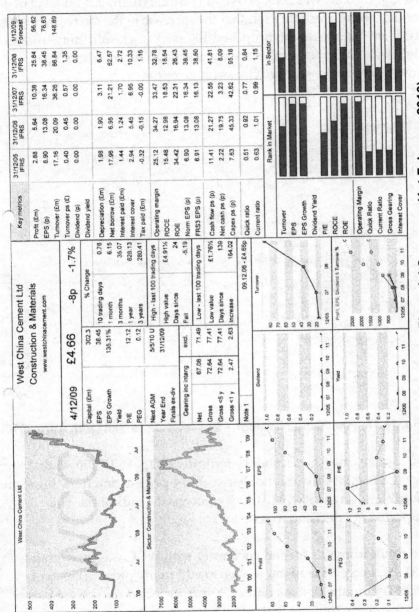

Fig. 16.16: West China Cement – Financial Summary (1st February 2010)

sell the balance. My notes are recorded on the scan of the Sharescope graph (see Fig. 16.17, below). Note that my primary decision to sell was that the PSR was 3.19, above my normal (high) cut-off level of 3.0. Another factor was that I felt that the increase in the share price was partly attributable to the proposed 100 for 1 stock split, announced on 9th March 2010. Stock splits are usually good for investors in a growing company and WCC was no exception.

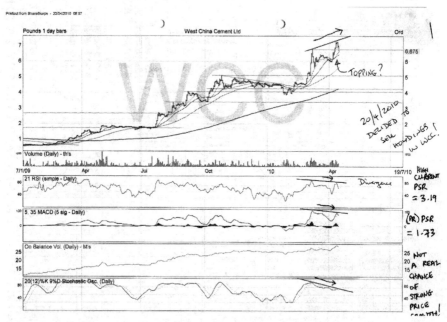

Fig. 16.17: West China Cement – My Decision to Sell (20th April 2010)

You can see from the secondary indicators (Fig. 16.17 above) that there was also negative divergence between the price action (new high) and lower highs on the RSI, MACD and stochastic indicators. This supported my decision to sell.

The result from this second encounter with WCC was an overall gain of 31.4%, in a period of ten weeks, to add to my previous gain of 110.76% from the first encounter. I have included the second part of this case study to show that, as DIY-Investors, we don't always have to invest for the long term. West China Cement was not undervalued or depressed — it was clearly a growth share. However, it was a company that I knew well from my initial investment (when it had been battered and bruised). I had also carried out extensive research and was therefore happy to trade it, over the short term, to take advantage of the likely rise in share price approaching the stock split.

Warning: *The whole essence of this book is to encourage you to make up your own mind. The point of being a DIY-Investor is that you decide what to buy and when, how long to hold and when to sell. The shares referred to in the above case studies are not recommendations. By the time you read this book, the situation or outlook for the companies featured may well have changed. Similarly, I may well have sold my holding(s) of any (or all) of them!*

17

KEEP YOUR PROFITS, LIMIT YOUR LOSSES

17.1 Having a System

It is easy, when you are focussed on the game of investing, to get wrapped up in the detail and forget what your goals are. Periodically, perhaps twice a year, you may find it useful to check your progress against your goals. You may want to go back to chapter 3 now and remind yourself what these were.

To reach your goals, one of the key issues, having learned how to make money by picking winning shares, is to have a system to keep it. This involves you learning how to keep your profits and limit your losses and minimising the erosion of your gains by taxation. To succeed, knowing yourself is also important as is the need to recognise that you:

- Must have and follow a logical system
- Need to continually improve that system (repeat successes, learn from your mistakes)
- Can learn to be a better investor
- Need to be aware of the basics of the taxation system (capital gains, income tax, tax-free gains)
- Need time to provide the leverage for wealth creation
- Can increase your wealth by regularly investing as much as you can afford

17.2 Keeping the Gains

If you are just starting out on your investing career, the chances are that you are in some type of paid employment. The only taxes that you regularly come into contact with are national insurance and PAYE (pay-as-you-earn income tax). If you are in a well-paid job or perhaps have been working a long time, your salary may have grown to the point where you are in a higher tax bracket.

A useful exercise is to take your P6O, issued to you by your employer shortly after the end of the tax year (5th April), and work out the percentage of your gross income that has gone in taxes. Be warned, this might give you quite a shock.

Next, carry out the following calculation for your investments, as a comparison, giving:

• Starting valuation
• Amount added
• Amount taken in taxes
• End valuation

It is in this section (investments) where the DIY-Investor can gain significantly. Growing your investments equals increasing your assets. Over time, this can become life-changing, enabling:

• Reduction of (or elimination of) paid employment (working for others)
• Greater time freedom
• Changed and improved lifestyle (n.b. this will be different for each of us)
• Greater financial security for you and your family

Taxes

Taxes, particularly in the form of capital gains tax, can seriously dent your financial performance. Capital gains tax (CGT) arises when you sell a financial asset (in the context of this book, this means shares) for more than you paid for it. Charges, commissions, levies, etc. on both purchase and sale price are set against the gain. In simple terms, the net cash you receive less the gross cost of the investment is your capital gain.

Each person has an annual allowance for capital gains that is exempt from CGT. Any system for keeping the gains that you have made should utilise this fully.

Dividends received from your shareholdings are treated as investment income and taxed at your personal rate of income tax. Note that if you are a higher rate taxpayer, this could mean at a rate of 32.5% in the 2010/2011 tax year.

Bring On the Self-Select Maxi ISA
For the average person, an ISA means a wrapper that gives tax-free interest earned on the cash savings within it. For us as DIY-Investors, this is not going to do the job, as part of our wealth creation. The money going in is taxed money (normally) and the rate of interest will only be marginally above normal savings rates, if you're lucky.

What we need, as informed DIY-Investors, is a self select Maxi ISA. This is a stockbroking account where any capital gains are tax free, when they're made, and more importantly tax free when they're withdrawn from the account. Every DIY-Investor should aim to have one.

Clearly, to take control of our financial future, what we need is a system that keeps some (preferably all) of our gains.

17.3 What the Wealthy Know – the Secret (Legal) Money-Making System
The concept, described in this section, could save you the cost of this book many times over and improve your financial situation immensely over your lifetime.

It is based on legitimate use of existing UK tax rules, an awareness of the differing forms of taxation and personal allowances, coupled with some very simple logic. The success of this system is based on two key principles — the power of compound interest and the importance of achieving market-beating annual (percentage) returns.

In essence, the DIY-Investor's Wealth-Building System that I am suggesting should look like this…

The DIY-Investor's Wealth-Building System

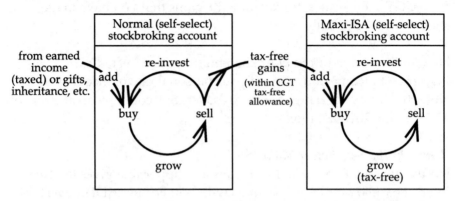

At first, you may be thinking "Why don't I just put all my money into the Maxi ISA straight away?" The answer to this lies in the fact that not all investments can be held in a Maxi ISA wrapper. This currently includes shares listed on the Alternative Investment Market (AIM) and shares listed on Foreign Stock Exchanges, where they are not "dual listed" on the main London Stock Exchange (LSE).

In my experience, some of the greatest gains, in percentage terms, come from the companies listed on AIM and some of the foreign exchanges.

So how does this system work?

In the normal stockbroking account (which you set up first) you place all of your investment savings and, of equal importance, add to it regularly.

With enough invested, you pick your shares using the techniques and methods covered in the earlier chapters of this book, or any other system that you decide to adopt or develop. From earlier chapters, you'll remember that I suggested £1000 per holding minimum so that costs (stockbroker commission, levies, etc.) are not an unreasonable percentage of your purchase.

In the first few years, you grow the value of this account until the capital gains approach the CGT threshold. For UK taxpayers, this is currently £10,100 for the 2010/2011 tax year.

Your profits, on capital gains from share transactions, will have to exceed £10,100 within the tax year to trigger CGT. Note that it is profits on transactions that count, not portfolio valuations. If your portfolio goes up from £30,000 to £40,000 with no share transactions, you have no capital gains. If however within a portfolio that goes from £30,000 on 6 April to £40,000 on the following 5 April, perhaps with several transactions yielding overall capital gains of £15,000, then CGT is an issue. In this example, your CGT liability would be £15,000 less £10,100 = £4,900 (taxable gain). This is then taxed at the rate applying to you as an individual (18% flat rate for standard rate taxpayers in 2010/11 tax year). CGT of £4,900 x 18% = £882 would therefore be due.

The DIY-Investor's Wealth-Building System would take capital gains, within your annual exemption limit of £10,100, and transfer this tax-free money into your self-select Maxi ISA. Any future growth within your Maxi ISA is then tax free at all stages — including on any withdrawals.

The balance remaining in your ordinary "execution only" stockbroking account continues to grow, feeding future tax free gains into your Maxi ISA, which itself continues to grow and grow.

As an Example:
For a DIY-Investor with a 20-year investment horizon, an initial investment of, say, £10,000 is transferred into the ordinary stockbroking account. A further £1200 per year (equivalent to saving £100 per month), is added. This gives a total of £34,000 invested over the 20-year period.

By transferring (tax free, as outlined above) regular sums of money to the Maxi ISA, the ordinary stockbroking account stays at a level where gains can be contained within the personal CGT exemption allowance (see Table 17.1 on the next page).

Table 17.1: Regular Investment in Ordinary Account and Tax-Free Gains Feeding Into Maxi ISA

Ordinary (Self-Select) Stockbroking Account — At start: £10,000

Year	Start of Year	Added	Sub-Total	Growth (@20%)	Transferred to Maxi ISA	End of Year
1	10,000	1,200	11,200	2,240	0	13,440
2	13,440	1,200	14,640	2,928	0	17,568
3	17,568	1,200	18,768	3,754	3,000	19,522
4	19,522	1,200	20,722	4,144	4,000	20,866
5	20,866	1,200	22,066	4,413	4,000	22,479
6	22,479	1,200	23,679	4,736	4,000	24,415
7	24,415	1,200	25,615	5,123	5,000	25,738
8	25,738	1,200	26,938	5,388	5,000	27,325
9	27,325	1,200	28,525	5,705	5,000	29,231
10	29,231	1,200	30,431	6,086	6,000	30,517
11	30,517	1,200	31,717	6,343	6,000	32,060
12	32,060	1,200	33,260	6,652	6,000	33,912
13	33,912	1,200	35,112	7,022	7,000	35,134
14	35,134	1,200	36,334	7,267	7,000	36,601
15	36,601	1,200	37,801	7,560	7,000	38,362
16	38,362	1,200	39,562	7,912	7,000	40,474
17	40,474	1,200	41,674	8,335	8,000	42,009
18	42,009	1,200	43,209	8,642	8,000	43,851
19	43,851	1,200	45,051	9,010	8,000	46,061
20	46,061	1,200	47,261	9,452	0	56,713
You Invested:	£34,000		Growth:	£122,713	£100,000	

Maxi ISA (Self-Select)

Year	Start of Year	From Ordinary St'broking Account	Sub-Total	Growth (@20%)	End of Year
1	0	0	0	0	0
2	0	0	0	0	0
3	0	0	0	0	0
4	0	3,000	3,000	600	3,600
5	3,600	4,000	7,600	1,520	9,120
6	9,120	4,000	13,120	2,624	15,744
7	15,744	4,000	19,744	3,949	23,693
8	23,693	5,000	28,693	5,739	34,431
9	34,431	5,000	39,431	7,886	47,318
10	47,318	5,000	52,318	10,464	62,781
11	62,781	6,000	68,781	13,756	82,537
12	82,537	6,000	88,537	17,707	106,245
13	106,245	6,000	112,245	22,449	134,694
14	134,694	7,000	141,694	28,339	170,033
15	170,033	7,000	177,033	35,407	212,439
16	212,439	7,000	219,439	43,888	263,327
17	263,327	7,000	270,327	54,065	324,392
18	324,392	8,000	332,392	66,478	398,871
19	398,871	8,000	406,871	81,374	488,245
20	488,245	8,000	496,245	99,249	595,494
Added, (tax-free):	£100,000		Growth:	£495,494	

The Maxi ISA, having been fed by £100,000 of tax-free gains (gradually) over the 20-year period (starting from the end of year three), grows to a value of £595,494 at the end of the period (assuming a growth rate of 20%).

With this approach, and investment performance, you have (only) invested £34,000 over the 20-year period and have gained (tax free) an investment portfolio worth £652,207 (£56,713 in the ordinary account and £595,494 in the Maxi ISA).

Using a SIPP

One other very important variation on this theme is to have a self-invested pension plan (SIPP). When you add funds to this, your stockbroker and more importantly the Inland Revenue assume this is taxed money (e.g. earned income) and automatically add tax at the basic rate. This gets topped up even more if you are a higher rate tax payer (through the self-assessment tax system), whereby the money can be added to the account at a later stage. For a basic rate taxpayer (20% tax rate), a sum equal to 25% of the amount put into the SIPP will be added.

So if £8,000 was added to your SIPP each year, from the growth in your ordinary stockbroking account, the money is effectively tax free (being capital gains within your CGT exemption allowance of £10,100). However, as mentioned, a further £2,000 will be added by the tax man. *(£10,000 of taxed income less 20% basic rate tax = £8,000 which when added to a SIPP has the tax added back by the government).*

The effect therefore is to give you a 25% instant return on your investment of this tax-free money. The investment can of course grow further within the SIPP but note that, with the exception of a possible 25% tax-free lump sum, any drawings (future pension) will be taxable as income in the normal way.

Note: *Consult your independent financial advisor for advice on pensions.*

To consider the effect over time, consider Table 17.2 (on the next page), where the money transferred (tax-free) from the ordinary account, has the basic rate tax added back to it.

Table 17.2: Regular Investment in Ordinary Account and Tax-Free Gains Feeding Into Self-Select SIPP

Ordinary (Self-Select) Stockbroking Account — At start: £10,000

Year	Start of Year	Added	Sub-Total	Growth (@20%)	Transferred to SIPP	End of Year
1	10,000	1,200	11,200	2,240	0	13,440
2	13,440	1,200	14,640	2,928	0	17,568
3	17,568	1,200	18,768	3,754	3,000	19,522
4	19,522	1,200	20,722	4,144	4,000	20,866
5	20,866	1,200	22,066	4,413	4,000	22,479
6	22,479	1,200	23,679	4,736	4,000	24,415
7	24,415	1,200	25,615	5,123	5,000	25,738
8	25,738	1,200	26,938	5,388	5,000	27,325
9	27,325	1,200	28,525	5,705	5,000	29,231
10	29,231	1,200	30,431	6,086	6,000	30,517
11	30,517	1,200	31,717	6,343	6,000	32,060
12	32,060	1,200	33,260	6,652	6,000	33,912
13	33,912	1,200	35,112	7,022	7,000	35,134
14	35,134	1,200	36,334	7,267	7,000	36,601
15	36,601	1,200	37,801	7,560	7,000	38,362
16	38,362	1,200	39,562	7,912	7,000	40,474
17	40,474	1,200	41,674	8,335	8,000	42,009
18	42,009	1,200	43,209	8,642	8,000	43,851
19	43,851	1,200	45,051	9,010	8,000	46,061
20	46,061	1,200	47,261	9,452	0	56,713
You Invested:	£34,000		Growth:	£122,713	£100,000	

SIPP (Self-Select)

Year	Start of Year	From Ord. St'broking Account	Basic Rate (@20% Tax) Added	Sub-Total	Growth (@20%)	End of Year
1	0	0		0	0	0
2	0	0		0	0	0
3	0	0		0	0	0
4	0	3,000	750	3,750	750	4,500
5	4,500	4,000	1,000	9,500	1,900	11,400
6	11,400	4,000	1,000	16,400	3,280	19,680
7	19,680	4,000	1,000	24,680	4,936	29,616
8	29,616	5,000	1,250	35,866	7,173	43,039
9	43,039	5,000	1,250	49,289	9,858	59,147
10	59,147	5,000	1,250	65,397	13,079	78,476
11	78,476	6,000	1,500	85,976	17,195	103,172
12	103,172	6,000	1,500	110,672	22,134	132,806
13	132,806	6,000	1,500	140,306	28,061	168,367
14	168,367	7,000	1,750	177,117	35,423	212,541
15	212,541	7,000	1,750	221,291	44,258	265,549
16	265,549	7,000	1,750	274,299	54,860	329,159
17	329,159	7,000	1,750	337,909	67,582	405,490
18	405,490	8,000	2,000	415,490	83,098	498,589
19	498,589	8,000	2,000	508,589	101,718	610,306
20	610,306	8,000	2,000	620,306	124,061	744,367
Added, (tax-free):	£100,000		£25,000		Growth:	£619,367

For the DIY-Investor using this system, with a SIPP, and having the same 20 years' investment horizon, the situation is:

Ordinary (self-select) stockbroking account
Initial investment		£10,000
Further investments £100/month		£24,000
(over 20 years)		
	Total	£34,000

Growth (@20%)	£122,713
Transferred to SIPP (tax free)	-£100,000

Balance remaining in the account:	£56,713

SIPP (self-select) stockbroking account
Transfers from ordinary account	
(from tax-free gains over 20 years)	£100,000
Tax rebate (assuming 20% tax rate)	£ 25,000
Total (tax-free) investment	£125,000
End value of pension pot	
(assuming 20% growth)	£744,367

**End value of investments
(assuming 20% growth)**   **£801,080**

[This includes the ordinary investment account (£56,713) and the SIPP (£744,367).]

Growth Rates
You will recall the significance of each percentage point of growth, over time, from chapter 3 of *Picking Winning Shares*. The crux of the "DIY-Investor's Wealth-Building System" is the actual growth rate that you, as a DIY-Investor, can achieve. The figures that I have used for illustration purposes are just that — an illustration. However, over the past three years, I have averaged a 46% annual gain in my SIPP, using the techniques contained in this book. I am confident that I can

regularly achieve gains in excess of 20% per year and I believe that if I can do it, so can you!

From this book and in particular, the description of my "DIY-Investor's Wealth-Building System," what you should absorb are the following points:

- There is no "top-slicing" of your investment pot by a pension fund manager.
- You control everything (including the rate of return, according to your abilities).
- The system needs time (it's not a get-rich-quick scheme).
- No tax is paid on the Maxi ISA model.
- The SIPP model has the bonus of tax rebates but income tax is payable on drawdown (except for 25% tax-free lump sums).
- Money can be withdrawn tax free from the Maxi ISA model at any time. You control this, although early withdrawals reduce the magic of the compounding.

My recommended approach is to have a self-select Maxi ISA account and a SIPP account. Both of these are fed from the tax-free gains arising from the ordinary stockbroking account. The more that you can put in regularly and the longer your investing horizon, the better the outcome.

17.4 Record Keeping

To avoid the tax man knocking on your door (metaphorically speaking), an accurate record keeping system is essential. This will apply to any account that you have, where the gains are subject to CGT. It follows that the same level of detail is not required for your Maxi ISA or SIPP (self-select) stockbroking accounts.

Successful management of the DIY-Investor's Wealth-Building System requires you to know your capital gains at any point in time. This is particularly important as you come towards the end of the tax year. So, for example, if you have realized gains, close to your personal exemption limit of £10,100, you will probably want to defer any transactions that will take you over the threshold until later (i.e. the next tax year).

18

WHAT'S NEXT?

Congratulations! You should feel really pleased with yourself to have reached the end of the book. We have covered a lot of ground together and I hope that my ideas have given you the confidence and inspiration to become a DIY-Investor. The combination of fundamental and technical analysis techniques, that I have suggested, should give you food for thought as you develop your own style of investing.

At the beginning of the book, you learned about the key elements of company finances and the different stages of the typical life span of a company. These building blocks of knowledge have provided you with a good basic understanding that will be invaluable to you as a DIY-Investor.

In chapters 6 to 10, you will have picked up the essential points that will set you up to make market-beating returns, by applying simple strategies that combine technical and fundamental analysis. In doing so, you have looked at how these techniques, when applied to low-priced, battered, bruised, or depressed stocks are capable of producing "share picks" that can double in twelve to eighteen months.

If you enjoy learning "how to" do things, then the practical applications of my methods contained in chapters 11 to 15 will have improved your confidence that you too can apply these techniques and become a great DIY-Investor. The Sharescope examples, used as illustrations, will have provided you with an important edge to improving your timing of purchases and sales.

I always feel that confidence can be gained by watching someone put things into practice. The case studies in chapter 16 are all based on real investments that I've made. By detailing the technical and fundamental analysis, together with the research that I undertook, you will have seen that it's not rocket science. You too can change your financial future by becoming a successful DIY–Investor.

You will, of course, want to reap the rewards of your investing success and chapter 17 revealed the secret (legal) wealth-building system that only the rich know. This clear illustration of how to maximise your tax-free gains will repay your modest investment in this book many times over.

What's next for you? One suggestion I would make is - to help others, please share the lessons that you have learned by telling everyone you know. In particular, help your children (grand-children too if you have them), to realise that investing is fun and can make a real difference to their financial future.

So, now that you have reached the end of the book, you're feeling (quite rightly), happy and confident that you can improve your investing performance. However, there is one more very positive thing you need to do ... go to your computer, look up

diy-investors.com

Then, sign up to join our community of DIY-Investors. It's free — and in return you will gain access to free research, based on the concepts that you've just learned.

This includes regular newsletters, provided free by e-mail, to help maintain your focus on this rewarding pastime.

If you've enjoyed this book, please pop over to Amazon.co.uk and leave some feedback. If you have any constructive comments for the author, please send them to

mick@diy-investors.com

As to what's next for me? Well, it's been suggested that I turn my DIY-Investors Diary into a book, in order to share my methods in more detail in a practical way ... watch this space!

Thank you for reading my book. I hope it helps you to improve your investment returns and achieve financial security.

— Mick Pavey
   (January 2011, Surrey, England)

APPENDIX 1
USEFUL LINKS

Website Address	Details
www.diy-investors.com	**diy-investors.com:** The website for people who want to take control of their own financial future. Free membership (sign up) for newsletters and independent research.
http://diy-investors.blogspot.com	**DIY-Investors:** My blog, where you will find me sharing my ideas, using the principles contained in this book.
www.sharescope.co.uk	**Sharescope:** This is the charting software that I use for the UK stock market. My choice is Sharescope Gold, which uses downloaded end-of-day prices.
www.tdwaterhouse.co.uk	**TD Waterhouse:** One of my choices for "execution only" stockbroker. Their company factsheets give a good snapshot of the key financial information going back several years.
www.stockbrokers.barclays.co.uk	**Barclays Stockbrokers:** My other choice for "execution only" stockbroker.
www.iii.co.uk	**Interactive Investor:** Good free "dummy virtual portfolio" resources here. There are also active discussion boards but remember my advice in chapter 12!
http://uk.finance.yahoo.com	**Yahoo (UK):** A good source of information and research for markets and companies.

www.fool.co.uk	**The Motley Fool:** Now more commercialised than the old "fool" site but nevertheless, still a good source for information. Again, good discussion boards. Also a good place to go if you are a novice investor, needing to find out the basics about investing.
www.advfn.com	**ADVFN:** Another good site for research, bulletin boards, and free stock prices, graphing, etc.
www.marketwatch.com	**MarketWatch:** A good site if you want to keep an eye on the US stock market.
www.proshareclubs.co.uk	**Proshare:** The home for investment clubs. Go here to find guidance on how to set up and run an investment club (if you prefer to invest that way).
www.londonstockexchange.com/home	**The London Stock Exchange:** Don't overlook this site. It has good resources for research and up-to-date company and market information.
www.hemscott.com	**Hemscott:** Another excellent site for DIY-Investors, with good free coverage of individual companies. Paid subscription also available for enhanced services.
https://www.orderannualreports.com/v5/index.asp	**Annual Reports Service:** Free company reports available by post. Alternatively, look on the website of the company that you are researching for downloadable (pdf) copy of annual and interim reports.

APPENDIX 2
RECOMMENDED READING LIST

Classic Books on Investing
Beating the Street, Peter Lynch (with John Rothchild)
Published by: Fireside (Simon & Schuster), 1993. ISBN: 0-671-75915-9

One up on Wall Street, Peter Lynch (with John Rothchild)
Published by: Fireside (Simon & Schuster), 1989. ISBN: 0-7432-0040-3

The Intelligent Investor, Benjamin Graham (Fourth Revised Edition, 1973)
Published by: Harper & Row (HarperCollins Publishers Inc.), 1973. ISBN: 0-06-015547-7

Security Analysis, Benjamin Graham & David L. Dodd (originally published in 1934)
Published by: McGraw Hill (sixth edition), 2009. ISBN: 978-0-07-159253-6

Super Stocks, Kenneth L. Fisher
Published by: McGraw-Hill, 1984. ISBN: 1-55623-384-1

Common Stocks and Uncommon Profits and other writings, Philip A. Fisher
(Hardback originally published by Harper Row, 1960)
Revised (paperback) edition published by: John Wiley & Sons, 1996, 2003.
ISBN: 0-471-44550-9

John Neff on Investing, John Neff with S.L. Mintz
Published by: John Wiley & Sons, Inc., 1999. ISBN: 0-471-19717-3

Contrarian Investment Strategies, David Dreman
Published by: Simon & Schuster, 1998. ISBN: 0-684-81350-5

Other Books on Investing
The Naked Trader, Robbie Burns
Published by: Harriman House Publishing, 2005 (first edition). ISBN: 1-897-59745-2

Hot Commodities, Jim Rogers
Published by: John Wiley & Sons, 2005 (UK edition). ISBN: 0-470-01498-9

A Bull in China, Jim Rogers
Published by: Random House Inc., 2007. ISBN: 978-1-4000-6616-2

Contrarian Investing, Anthony M. Gallea & William Patalon III
Published by: New York Institute of Finance (Simon & Schuster), 1998.
ISBN: 0-7352-0078-5

100 Secret Strategies for Successful Investing, Richard Farleigh
Published by: Penguin Books (2nd edition), 2007. ISBN: 978-0-141-03342-6

The Zulu Principle, Jim Slater
Published by: Orion Business, 1997. ISBN: 0-75281-012-X

Beyond The Zulu Principle, Jim Slater
Published by: Orion Business, 1998. ISBN: 0-75281-385-4

Books on Technical Analysis (Charting)
Investors Guide to Charting, Alistair Blair
Published by: Pearson Education Ltd, 2003. ISBN: 978-0-273-66203-7

How to Select Stocks Using Technical Analysis, Martin J. Pring
Published by: McGraw Hill, 2002. ISBN: 0-07-138404-9

Getting Started in Technical Analysis, Jack D. Schwager
Published by: John Wiley & Sons, 1999. ISBN: 0-471-29542-6

Books to Motivate & Inspire
Think and Grow Rich, Napoleon Hill
Published by: Ballantine Books, revised edition 1988 (originally published in 1937).
ISBN: 0-449-91146-2

Rich Dad, Poor Dad, Robert T. Kiyosaki with Sharon L. Lechter
Published by: Warner Books, 2000. ISBN: 0-7515-3271-1

Multiple Streams of Income, Robert G. Allen
Published by: John Wiley & Sons, 2000. ISBN: 0-471-21887-1

The 7 Habits of Highly Effective People, Dr Stephen R. Covey
Published by: Simon & Schuster, 1989. ISBN: 0-684-85839-8

Who Moved my Cheese?, Dr Spencer Johnson
Published by: Vermilion (Ebury Publishing), 1999. ISBN: 978-0-091-81697-1

The 80:20 Principle, Richard Koch
Published by: Nicholas Brealey Publishing, 2007. ISBN: 978-1-85788-399-2

Outliers, Malcolm Gladwell
Published by: Penguin Books, 2008. ISBN: 978-0-141-03625-0

INDEX

ABOUT THE AUTHOR

Mick Pavey is a Chartered Surveyor and Company Director, living in Surrey, England with his wife Maggie. He is a keen investor, specialising in combining fundamental and technical analysis to select, buy, monitor, and sell his investments.

He is a founder member of **diy-investors.com** — a community of like minded, independent investors, that share views and research. He also writes a blog, which can be found at:

http://diy-investors.blogspot.com

He occassionally posts short messages, using Twitter, at:

http://twitter.com/DIYinvestors

For relaxation, Mick enjoys landscape painting and sharing time with his wife Maggie (walking in the Surrey Hills and dancing [Ballroom & Latin American]).

Lightning Source UK Ltd.
Milton Keynes UK
UKOW031811170812

197702UK00011B/73/P